Getting Jesus
In The Mood

Anne Brashler

CANE HILL PRESS

ISBN No. 0-943433-06-1
LC No. 90-084011
Copyright © 1991 by Anne Brashler
All rights reserved
Printed in the United States of America
First Edition

Published by Cane Hill Press
225 Varick Street
New York, NY 10014

Produced at The Print Center, 225 Varick Street, New York, NY
10014, a non-profit facility for literary and arts-related publica-
tions. (212) 206-8465.

The following stories have been previously published: Wild
Strawberry, a Snap-on Button Shirt, the Best She Ever Made
(Confrontation); Getting Jesus in the Mood *(Ceilidh)*; He Walks on
Top *(The Literary Review)*; You Find a Prince *(Ohio Journal)*;
Vibrations Which Rumble Like Thunder *(Southern Humanities
Review)*; The Fun (forthcoming in *Cimarron Review*); #35-1460!
(StoryQuarterly); Do It *(Dark Horse)*; Duck Blind *(Conditions)*.

Photograph by F. Podulka
Cover photographs hand-tinted by Mary Bucher

CONTENTS

You Turn You Around

Harriet lit another cigarette, trying to decide whether to look like a matron or a girlfriend. Neither one seemed to be right so she decided to look like a sister. As Lemont wrote down directions, she watched him in a sisterly manner. I don't like him much, she thought, and then wondered if the tires on the rented Volvo would stand the heat of a sixty-mile drive in 120 degrees. They would be heading for Death Valley where people died if they didn't have water. She realized her curiosity about the chicken farm was morbid, but she was drawn to it in a way that felt comforting.

She watched Lemont as he drove. His thin hair, once blow-dried and carefully spread across his forehead, was now wet, and the separate strands clung together, looking like a leaf rake.

"I th-th-thought you'd like to come along rather than being cooped up in the hotel room again," Lemont said. When Harriet didn't respond, he laughed and said, "Get it? Coop? Chicken coop?"

Harriet said, "Yeah, well sure." She had hoped they'd do Vegas instead. "Unless you want to play the slots," she offered. She liked the nickel slots. All that clanker when you hit the jackpot. Also, she'd wanted to buy one of those jersey jumpsuits she'd seen in the stores. A fuchsia one maybe, with a dark red cherry belt. Lemont liked red. He always said so when he saw a young blonde wearing that color. The tighter the dress the better.

"You can do it tomorrow," Lemont said. He gunned the motor, heading south.

Harriet was glad she'd brought along two packs of cigarettes instead of one and wondered how long she could go without water after the tire blew out. They always did in rented cars when you drove too long on hot pavement. She wondered if Lemont knew how to change a tire. Now she wasn't sure. And where would she stand while he did this? "I'd get under the car," she said.

"W-w-what?" Lemont asked. He rubbed his left arm where the sun was turning the skin pink under a layer of black hair. "You got a rag or something?" he asked. "Got to cover this arm."

"If we had a flat, I'd get under the car for shade," she said. She wondered if they would be more likely to have a flat now that she'd mentioned it. She started to wind her watch and then saw that it had stopped.

When she noticed the sagebrush and sand whipping by, she glanced at the speedometer which registered seventy miles an hour. "Slow down," she said. "You're going too fast." God, she could hate him now, and herself, too. "Will they let me in?" she asked.

"Sure. Nice cold beer. Mahogany tables and chairs shined like glass, old-fashioned prints of Varga girls, posters of old pistols."

"How do you know?"

"Research," Lemont said. "Why don't you turn on the radio or something?"

Harriet turned the dial but there was only static. "Too hot for music to get way out here," she said. She lit a cigarette and concentrated on clumps of bristly bushes along the road, determined not to say another word. She was glad she'd worn her white slacks the day before so they weren't like just being cleaned for this trip. When they had the flat, at least she'd have had one good day in them.

They drove through mountains, a two-lane road now, and Lemont kept the needle under seventy except when his foot was off the pedal. "C-c-coasting isn't the same as speeding," he said. "You have more control when you coast." He clamped his teeth together.

God, not that again, Harriet thought. Something strange there, a kind of pain. The ensuing whistle breathed long and whispery, tuneless.

At Pahrump, the gas station attendant said, "You turn you around and go until you see you a dirt road name Hartland and then you take you a right and follow it until you come to the end of the road."

"Are th-th-there any places open before that?" Lemont asked as he cupped his hand over his mouth.

"Nope," the man said. As he looked Harriet up and down with eyes that bulged from a thyroid condition, Harriet made the sister image hang around until the Volvo was back on the road again.

"We'll be there in no time," Lemont said. The whistle was back like a long sigh.

"Good," Harriet said. She figured, with luck, she'd be having a beer at the Mardi Gras no later than five-thirty. In her mind, they were already going back.

They passed a pet cemetery with miniature headstones over the graves, a tuft with thin green grass trying to grow; then the dirt road became nothing but dust and stubs of growth that looked like charcoal, as if the entire place had once been burned to the ground.

"You sure they'll have cold beer?" Harriet asked.

"You'll see," Lemont said.

The Chicken Farm was at the end of the road. Four double trailers were surrounded by an electric fence. Red light bulbs dangled from the top of the fence and trailed around gutters which jutted out from the trailers.

Lemont turned off the ignition. "Okay," he said. "This is it."

When Harriet climbed out, she was shocked at how much hotter it was there in Pahrump than it had been in Vegas. The desert breeze blew down her neck, blew her hair back, and made her sunglasses feel hot on her nose. She removed her hat and swung it in front of her like a fan.

A huge sign dangled on the fence. RING THE BELL AND WAIT. Lemont made a grin-smile as he pushed the buzzer. His lips puckered but no whistle came out.

A scrawny woman in tight blue jeans opened the front door. Her hair was pulled back in a tight pony tail. "What can I do for you, Sir?" she asked. Her eyes had a closed-out look which, Harriet suspected, took in everything. She decided the sister image wasn't working, that nothing was, that she didn't care anymore. As she stared at the woman, she felt more naked than she ever had in her entire life. All around was nothing but dead dry branches.

Lemont grinned and shouted in his squeaked voice, "I'm l-l-looking for some chicken-n-n-n." It sounded as if his whistle had been trapped in his stomach.

As the woman smiled, her nose reddened until it looked like a round red cherry.

"I want to eat some!" Lemont shouted. He leaned forward, hungry-like, hooking his fingers in the steel fence.

The woman shook her pony tail. "The girls aren't ready," she said, denying the sign above her on which was printed in bold red letters, OPEN TWENTY FOUR HOURS, SEVEN DAYS A WEEK EXCEPT CHRISTMAS.

"But I'm hungry!" Lemont shouted. The squeak was gone.

Harriet thought, the bastard; he's forgotten I'm here. I'll never get a cold beer in there. A wave of self-pity swept over her and mingled with the hot breeze.

"Well, okay," Pony Tail said. "But the lady can't come in."

Lemont was a ball of action all at once. He ran to the car, unlocked the door and signaled for Harriet to get back in. "I'll only be a minute," he said. Perspiration poured down his face and his bangs had matted together, forming a thin mop on one side of his forehead. He pushed the hair back and it stuck up there like a peacock's tail.

"Well, turn on the air-conditioning then," she said. "Unless you expect me to crawl under the car." As the red lights around the gutters suddenly sparkled, she had an attack of self-loathing so strong it nearly blinded her. She climbed inside the car and slammed the door. "Goddamn goddamn goddamn," she said and pounded her fists on the dashboard.

The woman and Lemont remained on the steps leading to the front door. They talked and pointed in the direction of the Volvo. The woman drew her index finger against her throat and nodded. After a while, Lemont motioned for Harriet to follow.

"Sh-sh-she changed her mind," he said. "Didn't want you getting asphyxiated." His face was deep red now; his voice caught in his throat, making a wheezing noise.

Inside, the parlor was cool. Brown leather overstuffed chairs, a long brown plaid sofa. No shiny mahogany looking like glass, no trays around indicating cold beer. Not even a poster of anything except in a recessed wall facing the front door—a crude picture depicting an oversized rooster chasing a naked girl with large round breasts that looked as if they were flying.

Harriet sat on the end of the sofa and crossed her legs at the knees, carefully creasing down the fold-line of her white slacks. At first she wasn't going to look at Lemont but then decided she would. What does a man look like when he's buying a girl?

Lemont sat on the edge of a chair in a corner of the parlor. His eyes were dark, like a chicken hawk's. He clamped his teeth together and put on his grin smile.

Harriet hoped he wouldn't whistle.

The woman with the pony tail went into another room and led out four girls on an invisible string. When the girls lined up, she said, "Okay, now, introduce yourselves." Her voice had the flat impersonal sound of a telephone operator when she says, "Number, please?"

The girls wore bathing suits, playboy bunny costumes, each one a different color; fuchsia, emerald green, periwinkle blue, canary yellow. The girls gazed at Lemont, not moving an eyelash. Harriet was glad they didn't look at her. It was as if she were a piece of furniture, a lamp slightly out of place, nothing more. She imagined herself a pillow, blending into the sofa.

"My name is Cathy," the first one said. She made herself look ugly by not smiling.

"I see," Lemont said. He was leaning forward now, as if hard of hearing. His face had the expectant look of a child about to open a present.

"My name is Toby." The second girl wore heavy make-up and looked as if she wanted the trick. "Take me," her eyes said. "I'll be good. You'll see."

"I see," Lemont said. "And you?" The third girl said, "Mary," in a low whisper. She looked barely in her teens. Harriet wondered if Pony Tail could be her aunt, keeping the kid at summer camp.

The fourth girl shook her long black hair and said, "My name is Kewpee. If you pick me, I'm just a doll." Her voice had a giggle to it, a little girl playing patacake.

Lemont pointed to the second one. "I d-d-didn't catch your name," he said. He cupped a hand behind his ear and leaned forward so far in his seat, it looked as if he might tip over.

"Toby," she said.

"I want you," he said.

Lemont followed Toby through a doorway, scooting behind her as if ready to break into a gallop if she got too far ahead. The bangles and beads hanging from strings in the doorway rattled. The other girls left one by one.

Harriet looked around the parlor, not daring to move from the couch. Nothing to read, no TV, an empty aquarium in one corner of the room. She listened for noises but there were none; no voices whispering from the other rooms, no bed springs squeaking. She sniffed for a scent of perfume, even Lysol or furniture polish, but there was nothing she could identify; just an empty aquarium, rust forming on the inside of the tank.

She was startled when Pony Tail slipped back into the room and placed a cup of hot coffee by her elbow. "Do you drink it black?" she asked.

"Yes," Harriet said. "Thank you." So close in age, they could have been sisters. She thought of her older sister, Sarah. Sarah was the shaker and doer, always had been. She used to try to get Harriet to move faster, shake a leg, but Harriet never did, never tried. Sarah called her a leaf. "A leaf in the wind," she'd say. "Poor Harriet."

Pony Tail disappeared as silently as she had entered, before Harriet could thank her for not keeping her outside in the car. Harriet looked around the room more closely, trying to find details which would tell about the place, but she didn't see anything.

In the car going back, Harriet wished Lemont would drive faster.

"She thought you were my w-w-wife," Lemont said. "A wife who was dying or something. If she really loved him, she'd want whatever he wanted, wouldn't she?"

"What's that got to do with anything?" Harriet asked. She leaned forward, pushing. "We almost there?" she asked. For a moment, she was thinking she could get the car to do something.

Wild Strawberry, a Snap-on Button Shirt, the Best She Ever Made

IS THERE A WOMAN OUT THERE WITH NO PROBLEMS, SOME INCOME, FORTY-FIVE TO FIFTY-THREE YEARS OLD THAT LIKES RANCH AND DESERT LIVING AND COULD STAND A FIFTY-THREE-YEAR-OLD BACHELOR?

Would you answer a ad like that? I didn't expect nothing, the way things were with me but damn, I was lonely so I put that ad in the *Farmer's Gazette* and waited to see what'd happen. Scare't hell out of myself after sending it off. Twenty-six women answered, one a churchie and one a crank. Some thought I owned a ranch, some thought I had money, and some had money, leastwise they said they did.

The women were anywheres from forty to sixty-nine in age, all good cooks, they said, and interested. All were lonely and one said would I send her a list of applicants I wasn't using, said every human, male or female, needed a wife. Most sent pictures which I put on the wall, sticking them up with thumbtacks so's I could look them over while getting supper. One dame pestered the *Gazette* so bad wanting my address right away, I put a lock on the door of my trailer.

Harris is my handle, gone by it fifty-three years and six months. Been so long since I used my real name, probably couldn't spell it right anyway without looking up my birth certificate. I wear glasses for reading, am deaf in one ear, and got a trick knee, result of missing a boxcar and dragging on the rails. I've been a drunk and a bum most of my life but am trying AA now and that helps. I take Antabuse and that's a sure bet. Drank one time after

Antabuse and it was a toss-up which way I'd go. It's been sixteen months since I quit the booze; now I have a good job and plan to stick. I work a fourteen-thousand-acre ranch with other hands, but I'm the only one running the tractor.

Family, hell, I ain't had none to speak of for forty years, my choice, not theirs. Don't even know what happened to my sister. They split us up so we weren't like family anymore. I was a kid got hit whenever somebody looked at me. My Aunt Rhody took me when my old man went on the bum; she was a Holy Roller who hit kids whenever God told her to. Don't have nothing against religion but Christ, I hate a mean God. He sure told her to hit me a lot of times when I didn't do nothing wrong. Some people just born crazy, I guess. Old Rhody near kilt me with the razor strop. She puffed up when she got excited and I bet today she's dead, dying from an old puffing-belly anger. "Harris," she'd say, "you-all get down to that cellar before I get any madder." And she'd be puffing all the while, blowing herself up like a big white whale. I near killed her one time, she hit me so hard, but I packed up and left instead. I was more scared of my temper than feared of her, her whomping me with a strop on my bare skin and me eying the cellar for things to kill her with. Be about thirteen at the time, been on the bum ever since. Been all over, all the best alleys in big cities—Denver, Boston, San Diego; you name them, I been there.

Twenty-five letters, twenty-one pictures I hung on the wall and studied every night over meals. Some of the women were good-looking but not quite right and I'd go drifting back, remembering where I'd been, how I got where I was, not much hoping but not giving up, either. On a Thursday, last summer, Esther's letter was the twenty-sixth to come in the mail. When I picked up the envelope, I knew this was it. A feeling beat through the envelope, burned my hands. No picture and just four lines long. *I be fifty-three come next August and wear glasses. I lived in the desert all my life. Not much money, though. Esther.*

Saturday I called and told her I'd be down. Esther lived in

Princeville, two hundred and thirty miles away. I was scared for sure, driving those miles, wondering whether or not a decent woman would take me on, me being so long without one. After giving up booze, checking out the hoots I used to drink with, they didn't want anything to do with me. "Harris," they'd say, "you be clean and sober now, you ain't no fun atall." And I'd look at their fat bloated bellies and crusted eyes and be tempted for sure but not much. People look different when you're sober. And the stink. I never smelt the stink before, beings I stunk just as much in those days.

Every town I hit, driving to Esther's place, I bought something; new socks, new belt, a new ten-gallon from an old Indian. One town, there was this park, red geraniums and white begonias all setting around in clay pots and a little kid selling them, you could tell, for his grandmother. She sat in a rocking chair, rocking away and listening, pretending she wasn't. I bought the flowers to dude up the trailer. I still got the geraniums and they blooming to beat the band. The begonias tried but they ain't what you'd call a desert flower.

Esther had a nice little house and yard with morning-glories stringed on chicken wire, a porch with a swing—the old-fashioned kind, wooden, hangs from the ceiling, painted green, I noticed; all new paint as if she'd done it after I called. That made me feel good but still, I passed the house twice before I drove in. I was pleasantly surprised. She ain't but a wisp of air blown into a bundle of sticks and is sixty-five. Said she wanted to tell me that right off, her being older. "Harris," she said, "I done buried three husbands already and I'm tired of going to funerals." So I told her about how I used to drink but don't anymore.

We talked from six in the evening to two in the morning and then I drove home wondering what she thought about me. Her age didn't bother me none; she's a young sixty and I'm a weather-beaten fifty. We balance, if you know what I mean. She's just a tiny little thing, come up to my shoulder, smells like a meadow in springtime. And she's got the dearest little twinkle and a line of crow's-feet from laughing and a tough hide shows she spent years in the sun. And pretty? She's the most beautiful woman I ever seen, bar none.

After some phone calls and more letters, Esther came up and stayed Labor Day weekend. I'd worked to fix up the place; whitewashed the outhouse and laid a cover of new hay over the manure. Put new ticking in a mattress and fixed the pickup with shades in the back in case she wanted to think awhile before crawling into bed with me. I'd moved the pictures of the ad ladies off the wall and put them in a basket with other bills.

I found some cacti with pink flowers on them out on the range and painted a couple deadwood pieces, made a roadrunner and painted it red and yellow to cheer up inside the pickup. She slept there the first night and then said, "Hell, Harris, we got no business playing games. You want me in your bed or don't you?" The old trailer bounced off its footings that night, I'll tell you, and the next day I checked the underpinnings. Esther laughed when I told her what I was doing, her laugh lines working all crinkly and glad, and she started bread going, the smell hitting me in the pit of my stomach when the bread started rising and she put it in the oven to bake. God, baking bread in a hot oven has to be the best smell in the world. I near cried as I put extra underpinnings around the old ones. We live together, we going to need a good foundation, I said. I was already half in love, her laugh following me everywhere and the baking bread smell in my pocket. Later, she told me she'd got halfway to my trailer and almost kept going. I have three acres of yard—most of it in front— and the nearest neighbor is two miles away. By the time she was ready to leave, she'd already got me to borrow the tractor from my boss, turn up dirt and weeds and set two furrows for planting. "But Esther," I said. "Sand'll fill them furrows in no time." God, I hate sand. It sticks in your teeth, gets in your eyes, piles up against buildings like dirty snow. You can't wash it out of your clothes, sticks in the seams. Gets under your fingernails, too, like an itch you want to scratch but can't get to.

She said, "Now, Harris, just don't you tell me about no sand." Both days she'd swept off a layer of film covers the trailer, had the kitchen table waxed to a shine when we sat down to dinner. And coffee! I said, "Esther, that there's the best damn coffee I've ever had, bar none." She'd caught up a couple odds and ends of cloth, made some kind of doodad flowers and had them setting in a pot by the window, the sun shining through, making them real.

The next morning we had a fight. Esther'd been fixing things, dusting here and there and sneezing until her voice was near gone. I found her looking at the pictures I'd near forgot, the ones I'd taken off the wall. "You better look them over, Harris," she sneezed and then her voice turned squeaky. "I got no right to claim you 'til you've looked these others over." Some of the women were good-looking, I can't deny, in bathing suits and all. "You're the one for me, Esther," I said, but she'd got her dander up and left to give me a chance to make up my mind.

Made it up all right. Got drunker than a skunk on elderberry wine and with the Antabuse near killed myself. Called her four days later, near out of my mind. "You're the only one for me," I said. "I get confused looking at all them pictures and dammit girl, who'd want you anyway with that squeaky little voice of yours?" There was a long pause then Esther laughed, her laugh like cowbells in a pasture come milking time. "You want me, you got me," she said. So she came back and didn't look tiddleyboo at the pickup, went right for the bedroom instead, hung up her clothes and put doodads around; a pair of ten-point antler horns, some doilies on the chiffarobe.

It wasn't long after she said, "Harris, if you'd ask, I'd marry you." I near fell off the chair I was sitting on. I'd been driving the tractor alongside a slope all day, keeping an eye on prairie dogs dipping in and out their holes and was thinking how nice to come home where the home had somebody in it.

When we got married, her kids and grandkids came and we had an outdoor wedding. The preacher came from town and

21

we'd fixed the pickup for more sleeping space and served meals off the tailgate, Esther's idea, not mine. She found an iron kettle somewheres and I built a fire and we had the bigbangest barbeque Echoes Prairie ever witnessed. I'd made a ring out of a brass nail and she said it was the most lovely of her wedding rings. Said it'd be the last one, too.

After the wedding, the preacher said more words and then the town women filled our trailer with dried flowers, new towels, soap, and jars of homemade relish, everything a new married couple would need and then some. I was so proud and happy my buttons about burst. The most beautiful wedding, bar none.

Esther's load of relatives crowded around our trailer; half-breeds, dark and nearly white, her father old and Irish and Cherokee, her nieces and nephews full of zip. One kid short-sheeted us and I still owe him—tan his hide if I ever catch hold of him. And her mother, old and dark, gray braids hanging down in back, sang songs from Cherokee legend supposed to bring us luck. I kissed her many times, never once drinking anything stronger than coffee or the tea Esther had prepared.

Esther has three children, all married, and is a grandmother. Christy, one of her grandkids, stayed on after the wedding, slept in the pickup, and helped Esther with canning, skinning rabbits. One day I came in from the range and her and Esther was laughing to beat hell.

"What's going on here?" I said.

"Tell him, Gramma," Christy said, her little face blushing the color of geraniums.

"You tell him," Esther said, her laugh lines making a thousand wrinkles.

"I wrote that letter for Gramma," Christy said. "She didn't know until after I mailed it off." I pecked Christy on the cheek and gave her a bear hug. After that, we didn't say much but Esther made zucchini bread for dinner and Christy stayed up way past her bedtime, wanting to be around us, not letting go.

Esther's got me hooking rugs now and doing needlepoint. I'm

working rugs into designs, things I seen. One pattern has a picture shows a line of cars on a track, the black engine up front and the red caboose trailing in back. When I do rugs, Esther embroiders, using bone needles the way her mother and grandmother did. One time she put her work aside and rubbed her eyes, saying they were tired, but I didn't think nothing of it. We both joked about getting on into old age, but you'd never know it, the way the trailer shakes when we hit the sack.

One day we went shopping in town and I showed Esther my hideyhole—a false instep in my boot where I keep a fifty for bad times. "Harris," she said, "you'all just keep the money there and forget about it." So I hugged her like a good old buddy, thinking on what I'd buy her for a present. Never showed my hideyhole to a breathing soul; she's the only one.

Her stories could match mine back to back and then some. Her daddy was part Cherokee and part Irish and her mother was full-blooded Cherokee. Esther was born in a cave dugout with an adobe front. Six kids in the family and her and her little brother were the youngest, worked cotton with her daddy wearing a thin strop looped to his belt. They slowed down, they got their butts tanned. That woman, she's sharper than anyone I ever seen. Like the time we was riding cross-country in our pickup and I was sleeping in the back. Esther had her pistol on the seat like this sheriff told her once, an unconcealed weapon, and when she drove through town a roustabout stopped her at a crossing and banged on the door.

"I'm getting in!" he shouted.

"I don't think so," Esther said and she held the gun so's he could see she'd use it. And she would have, too, make no mistake.

She showed me how to knead bread. "You push the heel of your hand into it and pull it back with nothing but the skin of your fingertips." And when she'd do that, kneading, explaining, I could scarce keep from crying, she was that beautiful. "It's all in how you move the heel of your hand forward," she'd say, kneading and dipping, trailing her fingers back like soft balls of white gold.

One day I came in off the range and Esther was sitting in the kitchen, her head on the table, arms covering her face. "What's wrong?" I asked, my heart in a panic, scared I'd done something to hurt her.

"Oh, Harris," she cried, patting the back of my head, then moving my face up so's our eyes were staring at each other. "I can barely see you," she said in a voice so low I had to stop breathing to listen. "My eyes. I think I'm going blind."

She'd been making me all kinds of shirts and sewing flowers on pillowcases to beat the band, the pile of them neat and ironed in a cedar chest. She'd been making them and all the time she was rushing, knowing about her eyes, not telling me and me not suspecting.

We went to the hospital early next morning, my boss saying to take time off when I told him what'd happened. The preacher who'd married us waited while the doctors tested Esther, came back shaking their heads. They would operate, they said, but with the aggravation of sand, complications had set in. "Will she able to see?" I asked, praying in my head where nobody could hear; the words in a rush telling God I never meant Him any harm and for Him to do something to me but to leave Esther alone.

"We don't know," they said.

When I saw Esther next, her eyes were bandaged and I could scarcely see her face for the whiteness around her. I pulled up a chair and held her hand, still praying, still saying nothing. I stayed with her six days and nights, leaving only to go outside to alternate between praying and shaking my fists. When I got back to sit beside her bed, Esther said, "Harris, you wearing that strawberry calico I made. I can tell. Your voice is different when you got that shirt on." Wild strawberry, a snap-on button shirt, the best she ever made.

The operation didn't take and by the time she came home, I had the trailer fixed up good, new paint job on the outside, geraniums fixed up on the windowsill so's she could smell them. Fixed a patio, screened-in with a yucca plant and prickly poppy, all in a low tray with pebbles and sand. A brittlebush, too, some Indian tribe used to use for incense to bring their gods down closer to earth. I did that to show her we'd need a god of some kind now. She'd understand. We discussed where to put things so's she could find them while I was out ranching. She says she'll bake bread, too, if I set the oven before I leave. I bought her a fifty-dollar dog for company, him already settled in.

Before I left for work that first day after she came home, she said, "Harris, we're a pair, ain't we?"

"You know it," I said, glad she couldn't see my wet eyes as I closed the door.

Getting Jesus in the Mood

"Goddamn weather," she said and as soon regretted it, and said, "Sorry." Jesus was always catching her off-guard. "What I mean, Sweet Jesus, is if Jim was here, he could pray with me." She talked fast, hoping to cover up wanting Jim to screw her good after her brother Cy's kids went off to school. But Jim had gone to milk the cows. No matter her mood, she needed the loving. "Goddamn weather," she said again, only this time she didn't say she was sorry.

What she saw outside her window reminded her of home in Vermont, the snow so much like that at the old farm. And the loneliness was the same as now, and the feelings of being the odd one, the ugly in her family. They'd called her Clown because she tripped on things which weren't there. And she was fat. Not soft cuddly fat, but the kind of fat that made her thighs rub together, creating red chafing sores which had to be coated with flour and lard. She piled breakfast dishes in the sink then went into the darkened parlor where furniture was covered with shawls and bleached flour sacks. She hurried to the leaded glass lamp and quickly tried to light it. The flame sputtered as kerosene soaked onto the wick. She adjusted the knob, bringing the light under control, highlighting bright colors of tinted glass, blue, orange, green. She had loved the lamp since she was a child old enough to hold a match.

When the flame was steady, she placed the family Bible on the table then scanned columns of fine print, hoping to find a message which would guide her for the day. She held the magnifying glass up close, watched the small print jump out bold and large.

Once Jesus touched her and His touch made her fall to her knees. Now, she started to sing, humming low at first, getting Jesus in the mood.

"*We walked in the garden alone/ while the dew was still/ on the roses* . . . ," singing it like a love song, trying to trick Jesus into nuzzling her with his beard, and enter her as if He meant it.

". . . *for He walked with me/ and he talked with me/ and He told me I was His own* . . ."

She wanted to sing forever, but her hands were shaking and wouldn't stop. The Devil put thoughts in her mind. "Goddamn men," she said. "Goddamn Cy's boy with his little pecker wetting and wetting." The Devil placed his hands on her breasts and rubbed until her nipples were hard. And then he put his knee between her legs and pressed there until she ripped off her apron, yanked her dress up over her head and fell flat out on the floor. She let the Devil invade her, guiding him with her fingers, urging him on until the carpet burned against her bare buttocks. She spread her legs wide, urging him to enter further, to take possession. She thrashed about on the floor heaving and squirming and helping the Devil now, both hands pushing inward to soft wet places. She left a wet spot on the carpet, then prayed for Jesus to forgive her sins. She knew He would because He always did. She waited for Him to tell her that she was wonderful—which took a little longer, and then she got up, slid the dress down over her body, covering her knees, then put on the apron, tying a neat bow in back.

Again she ran her trembling fingers down columns of print in the Bible, searching for a verse to rule her day. She sensed that the Devil was still with her, scrambling the words. She thought of the bread Jesus made into a million loaves, and then she thought of the wine He made from water and slowly, slowly, the Devil went away.

Then, because Jesus was with her, she could think about her brothers and how they used to unbutton their pants, force her to spread her legs, and tolerate them until they were done with her, saying, "Nobody wants you, you Clown." They used her so they could save the reputations of the good girls in town. A Maddox boy never knocked up nobody, everybody said. Jesus had shown His anger for her two brothers: Cy had driven his car off the side of White Mountain and Potter, the other one, had choked to death on a chicken bone. "'Vengeance is mine,' saith the Lord," and she was grateful.

And now she wanted to do something to show her gratitude. She would bake a cake for Cy's children so they would see how much she loved them, how she and Jesus loved everyone. She threw ingredients into a pan and beat them together with a wooden paddle. Wafers, she decided to make communion cookies instead of cake. As she rolled the batter thin as tissue paper, flour dusted her face, her shoes, got up her nose. She cut wafers in the shape of diamonds, hearts, clubs, and spades, then remembered that playing cards were sinful so she ate the uncooked dough instead. Oh Lordy, Lordy. The body of Christ inside her at last. When He pressed against her nipples, He made them harder than the Devil ever did.

He Walks on Top

When my brother washes his sheets, I hear water splash against the tub. Aunt Rhody mumbles words and runs them together, praying. The wringer squeaks and I smell ammonia, which smells like my brother's piss.

My brother hangs his sheets on the outdoor clothesline. He wears a jacket, a scarf, a hat. He doesn't wear mittens because Aunt Rhody says that's what he gets for being bad. The sheets are stiff when my brother pins them on the line. Sheets fly like white paper in the wind. My brother smashes them to make them go straight.

I brush Jack Frost off the window to watch him. I want to go out, but I'm afraid. I'm afraid to go out and give him mittens. I'm afraid Aunt Rhody will say I'm bad, too. You never know what God is going to tell her to do next. My feet feel as if they are frozen in ice.

My brother's hands are frozen. He goes to the cellar. I watch from the top of the stairs.

Aunt Rhody makes him take off his shirt, his undershirt, his longlegged underwear. She grabs Uncle Jim's razor strop. She keeps it next to jars of applesauce and Uncle Jim's apple cider. My brother turns his back then she hits him.

Lord have mercy.

My brother doesn't cry. He says he never plans to. When my brother comes into the kitchen, he looks happy, as if he played a game with Aunt Rhody and he won. Aunt Rhody breathes hard, her face all shiny and holy. She makes us say grace before breakfast. We have to say it out loud so she can hear.

Afterward, when my brother goes to the barn, he steps where the snow crust is hard. He walks on top.

Aunt Rhody heats water for tea. She puts her feet up on a chair to help her ankles. She says, "Putting your feet up gets the swelling down." She says, "Do you want some applesauce cake?"

I eat her cake and it tastes good.

Everywhere My Father

Gramma said an eight-year-old girl shouldn't sleep with her own father, but my father said that a rolled-up rug down the middle made a double bed the same as two beds. I found a rag rug in the attic. Where we were was crowded because we lived in a three-flat and had to share. The rug belonged to Mrs. Kilpatrick on the first floor, but I didn't care. She'd never miss it, anyway. It was braided in colored strips from old torn-up dresses. I liked the red and black polka dot row, but the purple row was pretty, too.

After I pushed the rug down the attic stairs, my father and I rolled it tight. Then my father tied a rope round the middle. The rug felt like a body we were fixing to bury but Gramma said it looked like somebody's coat of many colors. She didn't remember the rug wasn't ours. My father didn't say anything. We put the rug the long way down the mattress then covered it with a sheet. With the bottom sheet tucked in, the rug looked like a hill to climb so I played a game: if I touched the hill, the sky would fall and our three-flat would tumble down.

That night I stayed close to my edge of the bed. Then I rolled to the middle and touched the hill but the sky didn't fall and the house didn't tumble down. My father didn't waken so I leaned on my elbow to watch. The sheets were loose and I sneaked them back. My father's pajamas were open and I saw a nest with a finger curled like a baby bird. I touched the finger even though I knew I shouldn't. The finger wiggled and pointed. When my father moved, I pulled my hand away. One of my father's eyes opened, then he covered the finger and cuddled it back to the nest. When my father turned in his sleep, he made the bed bounce. His breath was sticky like maple syrup. The smell was the peach-apple brandy he got from customers on the milk route. Sometimes he let me keep the empty bottles. Once he gave me a pink bottle in the shape of a lady with a big round skirt.

It was dark outside when I woke and looked for my father but he wasn't there, only the shape of where he'd been sleeping. I smelled smoke, then windows broke and people screamed and everywhere my father was calling. I tried to answer but smoke hurt my voice. All of a sudden, Gramma's face was close and lights from the fire made the room sometimes dark, sometimes bright.

"Geh up!" Gramma said. Her mouth was turned in like a dried-up apple.

"Geh dressed," she said.

I took off my nightgown and felt round for my clothes and a fireman came into the room. When he saw me naked, he said, "Holy Mother of God," then rolled me up in the rug and put me on his shoulder. He carried me out the bedroom and through the living room where Gramma was in a corner. She held up her fists like fighting and said she wouldn't leave without her teeth. A fireman dragged her to the window.

Water from fire hoses sprayed loops in the living room. I didn't see my father. I didn't hear him calling. When it was my turn to go down the ladder, I worried about people seeing me with nothing on underneath the rug.

"Don't look down," the fireman said.

When I looked down, faces and eyes were monsters watching. I piddled but the fireman didn't notice because a wall caved in with a loud crash and the monsters moved across the street.

"Look up," the fireman said. "You're easier to carry if you look up." I worried about my father, where he was. When the fireman set me down, he wrapped the rug tighter then it popped open. People could see my little hole. Firemen yelled and other men shouted until I thought I heard my father everywhere. A woman covered me in a blanket and said, "Come with me." She looked like the pink bottle lady with a big wide bottom. The woman half-carried me up the steps into her living room and my father was there with other men drinking brandy. I saw two pink bottles on the table.

Sometimes my father pretends he doesn't know me, as if I were someone else's little girl. Sometimes he pretends I'm a kitten or a fanglebird.

"Well hello there, Chicken," my father said. His eyes looked burned. I wanted him to cuddle me but knew he wouldn't.

Women were in the kitchen, their bodies rocking. A woman dried me off with towels, then gave me pajamas and said to fold up the legs. They didn't tell me right away that Gramma got sick when she was carried down the ladder.

The woman said "shush-a-la, shush-a-la" then put me to bed.

Later, the men said my father went out the front door and said he'd be right back. They said they saw him walk on by the three-flat just like he'd never slept inside that place.

The women said Gramma was not feeling well and that I'd have to go to a Home.

But then, if I went to another place, how would my father find me? If I hadn't played the hill game, we would still be in our three-flat and Gramma would be here and everything would be the same.

After the three-flat cooled off, I sneaked over to hunt for my china doll, my Heidi book. The three-flat was caved and smelled like wet clay and smoke was everywhere. I wondered if our bed was burned. I wondered if my father's nest had burned.

I climbed over beams and splinty wood and pretended I was climbing a hill. The mattress from the double bed looked as if the firemen had soaked it with water from the hoses. I knew my father wasn't there but I could almost hear him calling.

Knife

I started to get the knife when I heard my sister and my father argue. I sneaked into the kitchen while they yelled in the hallway where echoes made everything sound twice.

I heard my sister tell my father he should have been home where he belonged instead of out bumming around. My sister said she was tired of asking Mr. Peckham for milk and eggs with no money to pay.

My father didn't say anything. My sister said we'd be better off if he were dead.

Gramma shut her bedroom door because she didn't want to listen. I knew Gramma was reading the Bible the way she always did, her lips moving, the way they always are when she talks to herself.

My father said, "Nag. Nag. Nag. You sound like a wife."

My sister ran out of the house. The house felt empty with her gone, so quiet, like no one was home, not even me or Gramma, not even my father.

There is no place to run to in the country, only back roads and cornfields and maybe a barn for hiding. I would never run away even if I had to run for my life. That's why I tried to get the knife. I knew I'd be alone in the bedroom. It was nighttime and I was afraid.

My back was turned when my father came into the kitchen but I knew when he sat down. I knew when he put his heard on the table. I heard him cry.

I held the knife behind me because I thought I could sneak

across the kitchen floor, but my father heard me and all of a sudden he faced me, his face swollen and dirty, his eyes black and blue, his new teeth gone.

I squeezed the knife handle. Gramma kept the blade sharp. She said a sharp knife was safer. She used the knife for cutting up chicken and meat. We never used it for anything else, not even emergencies. When we moved to another town, Gramma wrapped it in a pillowcase.

I got past my father like I was dancing. I felt myself float as if I might fly out the door, down the stairs.

My father said, "Where are you going?"

I said, "Did someone hit you?"

He said, "Yes."

I said, "I'm going to bed." I slid the knife down to my side and kept moving, my father still watching, his eyes behind me. I wanted to turn and run to him but I was afraid. He looked like a stranger who'd come into our house. He looked like a small man I'd made up.

"Well, then," my father said. "Good night."

I didn't answer.

I moved the knife to the front where he couldn't see and slid it down until I felt the blade on my leg.

I went to my room and made sure the latch was all the way down. I piled schoolbooks next to the door. I slid the knife under my pillow then got into bed.

I thought of my sister and where she was hiding. I thought of Gramma praying and of my father in the kitchen, his body fallen across the table and his eyes black and blue, and of the men who beat him and stole his teeth. My father had been gone for so long and now he was home.

I slipped the knife out from under my pillow and kissed the flat of the blade. I ran my tongue over the dull side of the blade, then held the knife like a baby in my arms until I was singing.

I heard myself singing.

I'll Tell You a Secret

Some secrets you can live with. Others won't go away no matter what. They follow you around and get louder and louder until you want to smash them. I'll take some of the blame for what happened to Winfield Becker, but not all of it. His mother shouldn't have had him if she wasn't going to love him. I went to live with the Beckers when I was eight going on nine because the social worker said she wanted me where I could be with loving parents. Ha! Mr. Becker was about as loving as a piece of wood. He hardly ever talked and never once hugged me. He never talked to Winfield, either. All Mr. Becker wanted to do was play with Molly and rock her in that old rocking chair.

My Daddy used to talk to me all the time. That's what made our home broken in the first place. The social worker said it was broken and she was right. My sister and Gramma got mad at my Daddy always talking to me, and loving me. One night my sister smashed light bulbs all over him. He kept bleeding until Gramma called the police. After that, they sent my sister some place and put Gramma in a hospital where she wore a metal hat. That way, when she banged her head, she wouldn't get hurt.

Mrs. Becker wasn't so loving either. She could sweet-talk anybody she wanted and only took me so I could watch Winfield for free, and keep him out of the way so's he wouldn't wake up Molly. I don't think they liked Winfield after Molly was born. It was as if he didn't exist anymore. He was three going on four when I moved in. Molly was brand new. When the Beckers Baby-Molly'd this and Baby-Molly'd that, Winfield and I would take off for the dump to look for colored glass. Molly was going to be pretty, you could tell. Winfield was homely as an old bullfrog. He looked like Mr. Becker. About the colored glass: once I did something for Winfield which made him a sworn friend until death did us part. When Mr. Becker heard about the glass collection, he hollered at Winfield to throw the collection out. He said Molly might get cut and bleed to death. I sneaked the pieces of glass to my room in the attic and hid them under my bed. Then I told Mr. Becker he didn't have to worry anymore, that I had thrown the glass in the trash can.

Sometimes on Saturday, Mrs. Becker sent us to the movies so we wouldn't be in the way. At the movies, Winfield and I died laughing when everyone worried about Rin Tin Tin and if he would rescue the old blind man before he fell off the edge of the cliff. I didn't care one way or the other. Movies were silly because you could make them turn out any way you wanted. Mostly, I was Winfield's babysitter. I had to watch him and feed him and take him places. Mrs. Becker wouldn't let me touch Molly. She didn't let Winfield either. I guess she felt she was the only one good enough for a baby. Once she showed me how Molly was sleeping with two fingers curled up tight around her little thumb. She said if I ever saw Molly doing that, I was to stop her because that was how bad girls got started. I saw Molly doing it a couple of times after that, but I just let her be. It was none of my business since I never got to hold her anyway.

The main thing I hated about living with the Beckers was they ate tripe. Even now it makes me sick to mention that poison, but if I didn't eat it the first time, Mrs. Becker'd put it on my plate the next day and the day after that. She did the same thing with hominy. I think she did it to be mean. She never made pies or cookies or anything fun.

The day Molly got christened, Mr. Becker took off work and Mrs. Becker was up early ironing those little white clothes, lacy things here and lacy things there. And there was old Molly squeezing her thumb again. Mrs. Becker got mad and blamed me for not watching. Then, all of a sudden, there they were, the three of them, Mr. and Mrs. Becker and Molly all shiny and clean and ready to go. Winfield was still in his pajamas, whining and rooting around. Mrs. Becker gave me a nickel and said Winfield and I could do anything we wanted but I was boss because I was the sitter. After they left, I made Winfield take a bath. He didn't want to but I made him do it anyway. I told him when he finished he could come up to my room, that I'd be waiting. He liked that because the attic was away from the rest of the house. If it rained, you heard drops fall on the roof. Rain had a nice, peaceful sound which made you think of churches. When Winfield came into my room, his body was spanking clean. I was lying on the bed with no clothes on and I let him crawl all over me. He stuck his tongue in my mouth and I played milk-the-cow with his do-hickey. It was little—not nearly as big as my Daddy's. We took turns getting in Molly's crib and yelling M-A-M-A! M-A-M-A! Then we got dressed and went to the dump because Winfield said he saw some purple glass there. Every time I babysat after that, we did things that would make the Beckers mad if they knew what we were doing. A lot of times we took off our clothes and jumped on the Beckers' big bed and rolled around, hugging. It was fun.

Then one time, Winfield and I had a fight. He said he'd tell his mother what we did when she wasn't home. I pretended I didn't care; but it really did matter if he told. Mrs. Becker would report me to the social worker and then I'd have to go to the place where my sister was. That really scared me. If you ran away from her place, they caught you and put you in a room by yourself. That same afternoon, I took Winfield for a walk. We went into town and out the other side where there was a little park with a water tower. The tower had tiny curl-around stairs that went to the top where you could stare down at the trees which looked so small, just like they were toys. When we got to the top, I lifted him up on the cement railing and held him close around the waist so he wouldn't fall; then I told him I could push him over easy as anything and he would land on those tiny green trees. I wiggled him a little just to show him I could if I wanted. It was scary because I could have pushed him over and no one would ever know. They would think it was an accident. He started to cry so I held him closer and bent him way back over the railing—out into the open air. When Winfield started to kick, I almost dropped him. I pulled him back and slapped his face and said if he ever told, I'd push him over for sure. After that I bought him a strawberry ice cream and then we went to the dump to look for glass. I found a nice green one which I gave him for his collection. I found a red one, too, which I kept. It reminded me of my Daddy. I still keep it in my jewelry box but I don't look at it anymore. I just know it's there.

I stayed with the Beckers until I was eleven going on twelve. Mrs. Becker didn't like all those boys coming home after school, although she told the social worker she didn't need me anymore because Winfield was getting old enough to watch Molly. He was six going on seven when I left and Molly was going on four. The social worker decided I needed someone stronger to be my guardian so she talked the parson into letting me live with him and his wife. I guess, by living with church people, I'd be closer to God and that would keep me out of trouble. The parson and his wife were okay. They went to bed early and never once heard me crawl out the window when I had a friend who wanted to go to the dump. I saw Winfield a few times after that. He used to hang around football games and I'd say hello. Once in a while he'd come to the parsonage and we'd go off to look for glass. He was crazy about his collection. Molly usually tagged along. He told me they had another baby at his house. I said, "That figures."

One day, when Winfield and Molly were playing in the water tower, Molly fell off the railing. When I heard that, I about went crazy. I cried like I never did when my Daddy went away. The next day, instead of going to school, I went to the dump. I thought maybe Winfield would go there same's we used to when things got bad at his house. It was our special place, even though all the high school kids went there for necking and drinking beer. Sure enough, pretty soon he came. He didn't see me at first and poked around those old tins and broken bottles as if that was all he had to do.

"Hey, Winfield," I said. He said, "The funeral's tomorrow." And I said, "I know." He dug his toe into junk on the ground and pushed over an old beat-up sofa with stuffing hanging out. Underneath the sofa was a piece of red glass the shape of a heart. He kept turning the glass around, holding it up to the sun to see if it was a good piece or not. I asked if he still kept the collection under my old bed and he said, "Sure. Nobody knew about the collection except Molly." I told him from now on, wherever I was in the whole world, I'd look for pieces for his collection. I even promised to sneak him the blue salt shaker the parson's wife used on Sundays. That almost made him cry. Then he looked as if he wanted to tell me something so I said, "See you, Winfield."

And he said, "Well, sure." When I left he was still playing with that old piece of glass. It looked like a pretty good one, too. That glass didn't have all those air bubbles in it like the cheap ones have.

You Find a Prince

You go to college and drink beer with Chablis chasers. You play *Cardinal Puff*, chug-a-lugging until your eyes bug out. You have friends who laugh and play and talk about life over buttered rum and anchovies. You fall in love—once with Wally from the coal mines in Pennsylvania; once with Ezio, a rags-to-riches person who was stolen (he said) from the streets of Venice and adopted by a rich old woman from the Bronx. He is on a scholarship; you are working your way through.

You find yourself in a curled position behind the bar, on the narrow slatted floor stinking of stale beer. Zeke, the bartender, lets you sleep off the booze because you're one of his best customers. You bring in the college crowd that drinks pitchers of beer. You're a fun gal and everybody loves you. You're where the action is. It's World War II outside and people are killing each other. Your sister is a nurse at a prisoner-of-war camp in Germany. Your brother is in the brig for being drunk and shooting a cow in Africa. In the dark of night, he thought the cow was the enemy. Your father is on a desert making bombs. You smoke Lucky Strikes.

You do push-ups to stay in shape and ride a bike along a back country road rimmed with sumac and goldenrod. You love the challenge of hills and rise up to a standing position on your bike to make it to the top. You study when you have time which isn't often. You shrug and do a dance-y step and boys come along. You tease, making them confused and frantic, but you don't let them bed you down. Close, but no cigar. At parties, you throw light bulbs for the fun of hearing them crash. You are in a fight with another girl. You give her a black eye and she pulls out your front bangs. The fight is the talk of campus. You wear your hair in a pony tail, a fringe in front until your bangs grow back. You and Liz shake hands, refusing a rematch. Liz covers her face with charcoal and rides south with Billy who is black to tell his parents they are engaged. Liz and Billy hate each other but believe in intermarriage. They pack extra food and gasoline because Billy says you can never tell in the South. Their car blows up outside of Memphis.

You find a gambler, a numbers man, who stakes you for the funeral when your father dies. He gives you money for the trip; he gives you spending money, too. You throw a party at Zeke's; then you buy a black silk dress, patent leather shoes with sliver-thin straps, lacy black undergarments, which you wear to bed at night for practice. You buy a gold cigarette holder and bright red lipstick. You look classy when you climb on the train. Your father is in a plain pine coffin in the baggage car. They've given you his ticket. You wear a wide-brimmed black hat with red poppies on an orange band. A redcap holds your elbow.

You sit next to the window and practice looking sad. You see your father getting on a train the next track over, going the other way. But when he turns to face you he is somebody else. You feel a man sit next to you, his wide bottom spilling over onto your seat; but you continue window-watching, seeing your reflection, seeing the stranger next to you, his head outlining yours like a shadow. When he lights a cigarette you think he is your father, too, smoke rising in heavy curls; but later, when he slides his hand to the hem of your dress, you say, "Take your hand away, Mister, or I'll blast your head off." His hand stays and feels warm, comforting, but when it moves inside the skirt of your new black dress, you say, "I'll tell my father. My father will kill you." In death, your father protects you; he is real. The man leaves, running up the aisle, not turning round. He bumps into a woman carrying a child, and his ears turn the color of bright red blood. You smile secretly and wish you could stay on the train forever.

Your brother is at the funeral, escorted by a sergeant with rows of battle ribbons on his uniform. You observe the good looks of the sergeant and decide you love him; that you'll go to bed with him before he leaves. He reminds you of all the soldiers you said good-bye to in Boston, at South Station. You hug your brother, but that's all. He looks and feels like a stranger. He looks like a prisoner with his hair cut short, his toes turned in. You think about playing the Remember Game but decide not to. Remember when Dad threw lighted matches at the Christmas tree? Remember when Gramma slapped a Bible salesman because he called her 'Mother'? Remember the time our sister let Peckham's cows out of the pasture and the cows ran all over town? Remember? Your sister isn't there; the Red Cross had their wires crossed and didn't notify her in time.

Your head starts singing and you can't dust the song away. "*This old man,*" your head says, "*he played one/ he played knick-knack/ on my bum.*" You greet relatives, your hat tilted to show the poppies, their black centers winking like bright shiny eyes. Aunt Rhody is swollen like a balloon, Uncle Tracy has a bright red nose he's always blowing.

"*This old man/ he played two/ he played knick-knack/ on my shoe.*" Your father is clothed in a strange brown suit you've never seen. Too large for him, the flaps of the jacket are folded over, unbuttoned. He looks like an old waxed doll; two red dots like blisters on his cheeks. His hands are crossed at his middle; the rest of him is covered in a soft blue blanket with a satiny border. He looks cut in half. Your head sings, "*This old man/ he played three/ he played knick-knack/ on my knee.*" You think: so that's dead and you walk away. Later, you and the sergeant go skinny-dipping and you do it and you promise to keep in touch.

Your sergeant, your prince, says, "Do you love me?" You say, "Yes." He says, "Let's get married." You say, "Why not?" Your brother is getting drunk with Uncle Tracy. Aunt Rhody is reading the Bible to find out what tomorrow will bring.

Vibrations Which Rumble Like Thunder

Her husband is in the next room, rapping his knuckles against the glass tank, spooking the Dempsey, the aggressive fish he'd learned to hypnotize. She could visualize him using the handle of the green net to chase the Dempsey out of the weeds, its blue specks on dark scales shining while the back of the Dempsey's body lightened until it was shades paler than the fish it intimidated. Protective coloring; law of nature, law of jungle, law of the universe. She permitted one floating image of the darkened room in which her husband hovered, the ninety-gallon wall tank with neon lights casting an eerie glow on green plastic plants and rocks of blue and red. The frightened Dempsey would be swimming frantically now, in and out of weeds, trying to escape the net handle. The loud thump was her husband stomping on the floor, making, he thinks, vibrations which rumble like thunder waves to the Dempsey, the Silver Dollars, other fish trapped in their glass cage.

It had been six months since she'd watched herself and her husband move from their home in the country and settle into this little house, the place feeling old and used and battered by previous owners. While she'd packed in the country home, she'd felt the distancing as she sealed boxes and marked the outside with black crayon: bedroom, office, kitchen, shed. 'Distancing' was stepping out of her life while she hovered above the person packing and moving down below.

At her former home, frog sounds broke through the silence of night while early morning woodpeckers tapped out rhythms on poplar trees. They'd lived in the country home for twenty-three years, raised a family, watched the children grow, leave home, spawn families of their own; then sold the house to the Polanskis, a family of nine in need of more space. They would leave behind glass showcases her husband had built for his miniature circus carvings, a riding lawnmower, and Quaker Oats cans of emergency supplies in the fallout shelter.

When the Polanskis couldn't sell their house, she and her husband agreed to take it on trade. "It's a deal," he'd said, signing the contract. Since the closing date was two months away, she, to her later regret, suggested the new buyers move in gradually, thus expediting things later on.

The new family came every day. As they pulled up in their van, seven children swarmed across the backyard, into her garden bed of wild strawberries, violets, and buttercups. Mr. Polanski especially liked the glass showcases and was pleased with the keys her husband had given him for locking and unlocking. "Might start a gun collection!" he'd said, but her husband showed no interest.

As time went on she began to notice how Mrs. Polanski imitated her way of doing things; settling on wicker baskets, buying plants, asking for her brownie recipes, asking how she made tacos and quilts, and what neighbors she liked and didn't. At first she considered the imitation a kind of flattery, but then, when Mrs. Polanski began wearing similar clothes and had her hair cut short, she felt as if she'd lost part of herself. Just a thought at first, a string dangling from a loose button. Mrs. Polanski bought Laura Ashley dresses just like hers and looked better in them than she did.

She countered by wearing blue jeans and baggy sweatshirts, the kind Mrs. Polanski wore when she first looked at the country home. When Mrs. Polanski asked about bird-watching, she said she didn't notice any particular birds in the trees. "Just those old blackbirds, is all," she said, hoping the redheaded woodpeckers wouldn't start pecking away in the poplar tree. She didn't mention pheasants either, the way she and her husband used to scatter wild bird seed in winter and how mothers and chicks paraded up the hill.

During this time, her husband gathered his miniatures from displays throughout the Midwest and packed them away in cartons. He became so somber while doing this, she wondered if he felt he was burying them. He'd begun the hobby long ago, spending hours carving tiny horses, elephants, clowns, and painting authentically scaled replicas from the Dan Rice Circus.

Shortly after signing the contract, she watched her husband climb the hill where pheasants gathered, his back not as straight as it once was. She wondered if he felt he was being replaced, the way she did. Was he ready for Mr. Polanski's Flea Markets and drinking beer with next-door neighbors on Saturday afternoons? He'd talked about the fish tank Mr. Polanski had left in the house then, wondering if fish could take the place of pheasants. "We'll give it a shot," he'd said. "See what happens." She knew having fish for pets would be something strange for him, a fisherman from way back, up in Rainey Lake in Canada, the walleye going for jigs and large mouth bass going for rapalas and northern pike—big enough to feed a family—going for anything at all.

By the time moving day arrived, she felt as if she'd all but lost her old self to this new woman who'd taken her place. A distress she couldn't place hovered, threatening. As she settled into a routine in the little house, she lived mostly in the jeans and old baggy sweatshirts, sometimes not bothering to remove clothes at night but sleeping in them; it was so much easier than putting on a nightgown. She scrubbed fingerprints from walls, turned out lights in the crawl space, threw away wigs she'd found in the attic. The wigs were so filthy, she picked up with paper toweling, feeling a growing resentment toward Mrs. Polanski who'd moved into her nice clean place. "Darly," she'd say. "I mean, really!"

There were other things in the attic which she'd wanted to toss but her husband said to let them be. "Maybe someone left something for each new owner," he said. "It might be important."

"Who'd want a Jesus light with Jesus wearing a lit-up crown of thorns?" she asked but he didn't answer.

Before feeding the Dempseys live guppies, he now slipped into a green elf costume he'd found in the attic, along with a dusty photograph of Mr. Polanski wearing it. The costume had been made from a set of men's longlegged underwear with a drop seat in back. The green flap drooped on two sides where buttons were missing. "Oh my God," she'd said. "You're turning into a wimp." She leaned into chores with a zest that should have exorcised her growing anger toward the Polanskis, but didn't. "I can't help it," she said. And he'd answered, "Now, Sweets," in a way that made her enraged. He hadn't unpacked his circus display, the boxes were still in the shed.

When they'd moved in, the fish tank was coated with algae and slime, dark gravel that smelled like Limburger cheese. Her husband found overalls of Mr. Polanski's in the shed and wore them when he cleaned out the tank. She put away dishes, made notes of things she wanted changed, like the overhead lamp in the dining area—a composition of six balls which looked as if it belonged in the Algiers Motel on the corner.

As she made new lists of things to buy from old lists, her husband climbed a footstool to reach the bottom of the fish tank. He scooped up dark brown gravel with his hands, holding his breath until he transferred the gravel to a dishpan which he carried outside. "Smell must've killed the former fish," he said. He folded a handkerchief into a triangle and tied it around his nose.

"I know fish SMELL," she said, "but do they smell?"

He dumped the dishpan of gravel into an aluminum can then rinsed the gravel with a garden hose until the water ran clear. "We'll use the can later for putting our garbage out front Sundays the way the neighbors do," he told her. Garbage cans, empty cartons, and bedsprings crowded sidewalks on Sunday afternoons like attendants watching a parade. He wore Mr. Polanski's overalls almost exclusively now in the daytime.

Their tiny home sat in the middle of others just like theirs. McDade's Catalog House with its neon signs, the block-long Jewel

Food Store with fresh lobsters swimming in a tank, the OPEN ALL NIGHT gas stations, and the Algiers Motel made her feel as if she'd moved into a shopping center. She drew the drapes at dusk in case a passer-by would mistake them for living models in a housewares promotion.

"Darly, do I look different than before?" she asked over coffee one morning.

"Before what, Luv?" he asked. "Before the hurricane? Before the flood? You give me no reference point." He returned to a full page ad on pet supplies, found feeder guppies at a bargain.

"Before you became a little green elf," she said. "Before the Dempseys and the Silver Dollars, when we were back at the old house."

"Nope. Same old gal," he said. "Want anything? I'm going to the pet shop." He touched her shoulder and squeezed, a love pat.

"Not today," she said. He was into fish now, all the way. Sometimes, when he stood close to the tank, spooking the Dempsey, he barked like a dog and wiggled his fingers in the air—which made the Dempsey head for a hole in back of the plastic plants. He spent long hours in the pet shop. "They sure spend a lot of time doing nothing," he once remarked to a customer in the store. The customer looked startled, then said, "What else are fish supposed to do?"

"Never mind, Darly," she'd said at the time. "He probably blew the tenth frame in bowling last night." She wondered if her husband, in time, would go back to his miniature circus carvings. He'd once been a dynamo, selling ideas rather than solid matter. "The sizzle, not the steak," he used to say, tracking down carpenter jobs in the city, out on farms. He'd learned the craft from his father. When his father died, he inherited the tools, set up the jigsaw and workbench in the bomb shelter. A successful contractor by then, with enough earnings to retire, he became a circus master of sorts, traveling with his miniatures in winter months, putting on shows, pitching out his razzle-dazzle in nursing homes and hospital rooms. Where was that hotshot now? Where was the sizzle?

After a while she 'did' the house, buying a flowered bedspread, new wicker chairs and tables, painting walls, and changing carpeting in all the rooms, carefully buying 'baskets of such silken grace you felt them float from a table' as a writer once said; an oriental rug for the living room. She drove to shopping malls, feeling strange at first in her new role. Before long she began to feel life stir, not quite like being pregnant but something like that, expectant. She kept drapes open so that neighbors could look inside and admire what she'd done. Sometimes the doorbell rang and she'd answer it, telling the person inquiring where she'd picked up this vase, that picture, those flowers. If they stayed, she served chilled wine and cheese as if having open house. The home began to feel like hers now, but she still blamed the Polanskis for her husband's change in behavior. She bought new display cases for the circus pieces, but he didn't bother to help set the cases up after they were delivered.

Once she stepped into the pace of her new life, she felt buoyed up by the different directions and choices open, a surprise like an unexpected gift.

She never used to enjoy shopping, but now she went almost every day. "Where're you going?" her husband would call from his post by the fish tank. "Out," she'd say and leave. She tried nagging about his circus still packed in boxes, but he seemed not interested. "Oh, some day," he'd say vaguely, brushing the air with his hand.

She had the fun of buying new clothes for someone other than Mrs. Polanski's persona. She threw her blue jeans and sweatshirt in the garbage can and was pleased to see them hauled away, ground in the iron teeth of the truck. Her new clothes were more expensive and happier looking than what she'd worn before. She discovered she loved soft wools and glowing graceful silks and found a dressmaker who measured and designed and advised. "Join an exercise class," the dressmaker said. "Keeps you fit. Get your hair done."

So she stopped shopping and let the dressmaker create her

clothes and do her buying while she exercised daily at the Lovely Lady Salon. She jogged to rock and jiggled on the jiggle machine and rode a bike up a thousand miles of imagined hills. She closed her eyes to fill the hills with maples and oaks, the side of the road with goldenrod, sumac, and black-eyed susans.

When she sang in the shower, which was every morning now, her husband shouted something about caterwauling, and she realized her distancing was gone; she'd come down inside her own body again. She went to plays in the city, driving by herself—something she'd never done before without her husband; but he wasn't interested in plays anymore. Wasn't television good enough? At least PBS? Or why not come and watch fish? He'd let her feed them if she wanted. he fed them guppies often, watching the Dempseys open their trapdoors and gulp the guppies down.

"They look as if they just suck them up," she said, horrified.

"Those Dempseys, they're all fish," her husband said.

At last she unpacked his circus pieces, set some on display in new cases in the living room, arranged a ring of clowns around a red-and-yellow striped tent on the coffee table, but he scarcely noticed. He still alternated between wearing the elf costume and Mr. Polanski's overalls. She washed the overalls at night after he went to sleep. "But why?" she'd asked when he wouldn't change into his own clothes. He'd answer, "Oh, I dunno; makes me feel different, I guess." She played marches and circus music on the record player. When she went to plays in the city, she'd call him so he could fix dinner. One time when she telephoned, he said, "You've got to come home. That woman what'shername, the buyer of the big house, wants to talk to you."

"What about?" She'd all but forgotten Mrs. Polanski.

"Don't know but they'll be here in an hour."

"They?"

"Both of them. He wants to know if he can buy my circus. Seems he's taken an interest in woodcarving."

"Are you going to sell him the circus?" she asked, goose bumps rising on her skin.

"Don't know. Maybe."

"You can't," she said and hung up before he could respond. She hurried home and paused by her front door, expectant and frightened.

When Mr. Polanski met her at the door, looking exactly the way her husband used to—wearing the same type of gray slacks, a turtleneck sweater, even black horned-rim glasses just like his, she was terrified until she heard her real husband call from the room with the built-in tank. "The fucking Dempsey just swallowed a Silver Dollar," he shouted.

"Hi, there," Mr. Polanski said. "Wanted to see the old neighborhood, wanted to see what you two've done. Didn't like our carpets, I see. Didn't like our color scheme, either, right?" He picked up objects, checking out trademarks. Before she could stop him, he knelt before the coffee table and swept up all the clowns. "These are really something," he said. "No wonder he didn't want to show them to me before."

She feared for the little clowns, so vulnerable in his hands.

Mrs. Polanski's Laura Ashley dress with blue forget-me-nots was dingy and wrinkled as if she'd washed it with blue jeans. She gazed with surprise and wonder, eying the soft silk blouse and rainbowed skirt. "How lovely," she said. "Where did you buy those clothes and who did your hair?" This was not a friendly neighbor asking about a wicker chair or a framed print. Mr. and Mrs. Polanski swallowed people whole.

Get out, she wanted to say.

"I've chilled wine and the cheese is room temperature. Will you join us for a while?" her husband asked. The green flap on his elf costume was down again even though she'd sewn on buttons many times.

"Oh, they mustn't stay," she said. His empty circus cartons lay sprawled by the front door. "Who dug those out?" she asked.

"I did," Mr. Polanski said. "He told me I could," he said.

"They go, these stay," she said, pointing first to the amazed

Polanskis and then to the boxes. Her face became mottled with anger.

"But, Sweetie ..." Her husband seemed embarrassed.

"But nothing," she said as she opened the front door. "Sorry," she said. "My husband forgot he's giving a lecture tonight. Kiwanis club, I think."

When Mr. Polanski tried to hold the door open with his foot, she slammed it shut. "Good-bye!" she called. "This is our home now!" She locked the door and slid the dead bolt into place.

After getting rid of the Polanskis, she made a few telephone calls, persuaded her husband to change into his old clothes—with tie. When he protested, she threatened to drown the fish, chop the miniatures into kindling, then burn the house down.

They went together to set up his carvings in Walgreen's twenty-four-hour drugstore. Insomniacs and bag ladies watched as the druggist removed end-of-season tackle boxes from display shelves to make room for the circus. "Jeez," the druggist said, lifting out the miniatures with care. "Just like the old days in Appleton, Wisconsin."

"Best circus in town," her husband said, clearing his throat. He bowed to the small gathering and looked as if he might topple over.

"Go for it, Darly!" she said, clapping.

He shrugged, seemed to come out of a fog, and then, "Step right up, Ladies and Gentlemen!"

(She smiled, relieved.)

"...and observe the Magnificent Marvelous Miniature Mysteries gathered here before your very eyes."

A group crowded around him as he hopped on an overturned carton, light as a feather.

"The World Famous Burberry Circus," he shouted. "A Private Presentation at Wondrous Walgreen's, the Friendly Family's Famous Favorite place to shop...

"... A Monumental Modern-day Miracle, unchallenged in Size

Scope and Splendor ...

"... Terrific Terrifying Tigers, Daredevils Daring to Do Dangerous Feats on the Head of a Pointy Pin ..."

She hung back, apart from the gathering, seeing her husband in his old tuxedo and top hat, swinging his cane, selling the sizzle. She'd put him in the window now, where everyone could watch. She stomped her feet on the brown tiled floor, making her own vibrations.

The Fun

I used to watch from my bedroom facing Elrod's. With Grampa Mally's opera glasses, I'd see Elrod's shadow on the wall when he got ready for bed. He'd throw his clothes in the air like kites flying and then he did jumping jacks. I could see him, his arms reaching up and his hands clapping over his head. I'd watch Elrod's room until he turned out the light. I'd pretend to fly to where he was and we'd make shadow pictures of Easter bunnies. He'd show me how cows did it and horses did it and pigs and chickens and then we'd sleep together and his parents wouldn't know. Then I'd fly back to my bed when the rooster crowed. My sister had a crush on Elrod but he liked me better, he told me so. My sister wasn't real like I was, he said. We moved away before first grade so I never went to the school where Elrod did.

In the new place, Elrod stayed the same but I grew up fast so I could catch up with him.

The summer I returned to Aunt Jenny's and Uncle Ray's farm, I was fourteen instead of six and Elrod was a married man. I was shocked to know that Elrod was all the way grown with a wife and baby because I'd pretended that he was still fourteen, still in his bedroom at the end of the hall. I didn't connect that he and his wife lived in the little farmhouse now, that my old bedroom was their bedroom, and their baby slept in the crib Elrod used to use.

When Aunt Jenny picked me up at the train station, she said I could babysit Elrod Junior so Margie could rest. "Margie's not well," Aunt Jenny said. At first, I thought Elrod Junior was Elrod gone backwards. Then I realized Aunt Jenny meant Elrod's baby and I wondered if I'd drop the baby or hate it so I'd help some other way.

"You do the laundry," Aunt Jenny said. "and I'll take care of Junior."

Laundry wasn't any better than babysitting because Aunt Jenny made me iron all the workshirts and overalls Uncle Ray wore for milking cows, for plowing, for mowing hay. I was sad, too, because Gramma had tricked me into going to Aunt Jenny's in the first place. Gramma called my visit a vacation and everybody knew you didn't work on vacation. You swam and drank root beer if you got lucky and found money to buy it with. One time, when we lived in the little house, I found money under the stairs but Gramma made me hand it over. I never saw that money again so that made Gramma as big a crook as anybody, even though Gramma won custody when my mother died and my father went away.

After we got home from the train station, Aunt Jenny told me we'd be going to the cottage at the lake as soon as Uncle Ray finished haying, so I said I'd babysit at the lake. I was glad about the lake. When I was six, Elrod told me that the lake was Lake Cha-gog-a-gog-man-cha-gog-a-gog-a-mung-ga-mog or something like that, an Indian name that means *You fish on your side, I'll fish on my side, and no one will fish in the middle.* It's Webster Lake now.

That night I waited until Uncle Ray and Aunt Jenny went to bed. "You'll sleep upstairs," Aunt Jenny had said. "Up in Elrod's old room." They shut the bedroom door so I wouldn't see what they looked like in their underwear. I sat in Uncle Ray's leather chair and gave myself rides by pushing a button on the righthand arm. When Aunt Jenny and Uncle Ray started to snore, I found some red stuff and some brown stuff on a shelf and mixed a glassful with sugar. You had to hold your nose to drink it.

What hit me when I turned on Elrod's light was the smell of him as if he'd left his smell behind when he got married. Gramma said smells of childhood never leave you. The smell of pencils and the smell of leather from Elrod's baseball glove was there as if he'd never gone past fourteen. The white wall where

I'd watched his shadow was still there with nothing hanging on it. I opened his window and saw the outline of my old bedroom, the window, the little farmhouse in shadows now, but a thin moon shining enough for me to remember how it used to be.

I sat on his bed to drink the stuff I'd mixed in the kitchen. I wished I'd taken one of Uncle Ray's pipes but if I'd gone downstairs to get one, Aunt Jenny might have smelled the drink on my breath and she would've sent me packing.

When I started to get undressed, beginning at the bottom with shoes like Gramma said, I saw a long mirror against the wall. The mirror was clear with no splotchy parts so I looked myself over to see if I was prettier than my sister yet. I took a swallow of my drink, then put my clothes back on so I could undress slow and watch. Gramma never let me wear a bra. She didn't tell me about my period, either. She made my sister tell me instead. My sister said, "You bleed a lot and get pregnant if you do things you shouldn't be doing." I already knew about sex and kissing and doing it but I pretended to Gramma that I didn't.

After a while I took all my clothes off in a hurry, then I made my mouth into a big "O" to show how shocked I was. I pushed my nipples up to make them bigger, then got close to the mirror so I could pretend I was kissing Elrod. I could practically feel Elrod rubbing the back of my neck and kissing it. I could practically see his shadow on the wall moving toward me, then walking me over to the bed. We did this a couple of times, laughing. We were laughing. Then he did it to me the same as I pretended he used to. We did it for awhile, rolling over and over, then I danced to show him how I was graceful. I was kissing myself in the mirror.

Next morning Aunt Jenny yelled at me for leaving the lights on. And she yelled at me for leaving the window open so flies got in. I'd noticed prick holes all over the top of Elrod's desk. I said, "Did Elrod do his desk with pins?" but Aunt Jenny said, "No. He did the holes with an ice pick."

One day Margie and the baby and Elrod came over. I nearly fell off the chair when I saw Elrod. He looked older than my father would have looked at the same age. Once my father said he'd never get older. "Just wiser," he said. Elrod scarcely noticed me, as if I wasn't even there. Later on in the week when we went to the lake, Uncle Ray showed me how to jig for walleyes, leaving bait on the bottom like delicious food. Aunt Jenny let me help make powdered sugar doughnuts, too. I got to eat all the dough-nut holes.

Oh! We had fun! Just like the old days except for Elrod. He wasn't the same as he used to be. I'd say, "Remember, Elrod?" and he'd say, "Nah. You were just a kid back then." I liked Margie okay because she laughed like a turkey gobble and she let me hold the baby. I didn't drop him, either.

One day when it was so hot that loons and ducks stayed in the bushes away from the sun, Elrod and I were the only ones in the water. Elrod wanted to play London Bridge but before he dove down, he said, "I saw you the other night." He said, "You've got some piece of ass there, kid." He looked older than Uncle Ray, as if he'd raced on ahead, playing leapfrog. I tried to swim toward the dock but Elrod squeezed my arm and wouldn't let go. He dunked me until I choked up water then he made me stand so he could swim between my legs. I felt his fingers go up inside me. Then he pulled me under.

Hollywood

The whole town talked about how they'd never heard of such a thing. Whatever in the world, they said. Listen. I was ironing, the basket spilling over with the overalls and lumberjack shirts, and straps, and buckles, the clothes smelling fresh from the clothesline smell, the wind, and Mrs. Parker said, "You think you're something, don't you? You think you're pretty swell."

I kept on ironing, pushing on the board, hearing the squeak of the part where the underneath is, the legs, and I thought, don't listen, don't listen, but then she said it again. "You think you're pretty swell, don't you? Why can't you be like your brother in the army or why can't you be like your sister getting to be a nurse? Why do you have to be like your father? Your father is gone for good, isn't he? He's nothing but a drunk, isn't he? You think you're so swell. You think you're somebody."

She said, "Looka here. There's hay on your skirt. Just looka-here at that."

She said, "Homer was working that field by the school bus stop, just ahaying last Tuesday."

She said, "You lay with him, girl, and don't you tell me none else."

So I put the iron down on its heel and I brought the overalls' straps, the bib part, and the long danglies back up on the laundry pile and folded them, bending over, then I made myself walk away, not fast, not running, but dignified, not in a hurry, like a lady, and I walked from the room, then into the dark room which was the parlor with red velvet curtains and the sun slanting in and

I went up the stairs, still like a lady, even though no one could see me or never would.

When I got to the top of the stairs, my father's bed was still unmade as if he'd just gotten up for a minute and would be right back and I put my hand under his pillow, slipping my hand under slow as if, if something was there, it wouldn't cut me if it was sharp. But nothing was there so I went into my room and closed the door and wondered what in the world I would do and where in the world I would go and what in the world would become of me with no place to go to and wanting to go back to some place I'd come from before coming here.

I waited in my room until it was time to help with dinner, then I went downstairs, turning left then right, down the hall to the kitchen and Mrs. Parker was there, banging pans so I started to set the table and she said, "Leave it."

So I started to wash the dishes and she said, "Leave it."

She said, "You just go sit you down in the parlor and you just sit you there while I get you some tea. You just go be somebody, go be a lady, don't dirty your hands. I don't need a lady in the kitchen. I don't want you here."

I tried to look busy when Mr. Parker came in and sat down with the hired men. My father was gone. I knew he'd be leaving. I could tell when he was going to go, the drinking in the barn, his back so straight he bent backwards as if the world had tipped for him and was leaning on its side.

And sitting with the hired men, Mr. Parker, you could tell, was afraid, how he ducked his head, scooping up his soup with a slurp and then another slurp, the way people do when they're hungry and when they don't want the world coming down on them. I know he could see Mrs. Parker's eyes were red with the one eye seeing straight and the other seeing sideways as if she needed to watch round in all directions. I saw her, too. She looked worn out with the hired men sitting at her table, eating her food, sitting in places where children should have been, more than the one, with Homer a disappointment, and his wife,

Ruth, a terrible disappointment, too, so barren, and never in the world any grandchildren to pass on the farm to, no one.

So after I saw what Mr. Parker saw, I walked out of the kitchen, down the hall and up to my room again where I shut the door and sat on the bed. Then Mr. Parker came in after knocking and he said, "You'd better go on down and get yourself something to eat. You have to eat something." I said, "No, I won't eat if I can't work," all prissy and pure like I was somebody. He slumped out like he'd made a mistake coming into my room. So then I didn't eat and I went to bed feeling righteous, so vain, and thinking how I'd get to look like Joan Crawford, skinny with high cheekbones. But in the morning I went down to fix breakfast for the hired help and Mrs. Parker elbowed me, her elbows out like chicken wings, bumping me along, saying, "Shoo shoo, out of my way, out of my kitchen."

I waited until the school bus came. I waited outside. I felt Mrs. Parker's burning eyes, the clear eye and the one that didn't see straight. She watched through parlor drapes, an old woman who wanted to live in the city instead of the country feeding pigs and hired men. Then I got on the school bus and rode away.

At lunchtime, I went to Newton's Drug Store where Johnny Newton was jerking sodas and I said, "Give me a glass of water with a straw in it," and I sucked in my cheeks like Joan Crawford. I wanted kids from school to see me sitting on a high stool and sucking water through a straw. I wanted Shirley Hicks to see me, and her dead brother, too. I wanted everybody in the cemetery looking on. I wanted Lorelei Maddox to see me and her blind grandmother to watch me, and the teachers, too, and Miss Hinchley, the typing teacher who wore tight dresses and only taught the boys how to type, leaning over so their noses dipped into the top of her dress. And the principal, I wanted him to see me, and my father, too.

And now everybody knew I wasn't eating at Parker's, and I told it and told it so it would get around town some more, telling how I hadn't eaten, making the telling better each time. A brownie

Johnny Newton gave me was the last thing I ate.

All the time in school, in homeroom, on the playground, kids tried to break me down, as if, if they could, they would break me, my friends even, Shirley Hicks and Lorelei Maddox, brought me egg salad sandwiches and fresh peaches ready to eat. But I closed my mouth and after the third day, it was easy not eating, and I felt wobbly the way my father looked when he'd been drinking.

But then I got frightened and people were getting tired of the story and how they'd never heard of such a thing, so I told Miss Doyle, my French teacher who had told me I was flunking her class, and she took me back to where she was boarding in town, with poor people. So I went home with her and they took me, the poor man and the poor woman who kept State children who had no other home. They said, "If children don't have somebody, who will love them?" They sat me down for grits with homemade syrup. "Whatever in the world," they said. "Whatever in the world."

So then the poor man said, "Well now, we'll go get them clothes what belong to you." So we drove up the hill, up around the covered bridge till we were in Parkers' drive and Mrs. Parker was waiting on the porch step, the top one, with her arms crossed and her crooked eye looking at the hills and her straight eye looking at me.

She said, "If you step on that bottom step, I'll get you arrested."

She said, "Homer and Mr. Parker'll be right back."

She said, "They'll mow you down."

The man said, "Woman, step aside," not loud but like he meant for her to move. Then he said, "Go get your things, child. You're moving."

I stepped from the car and went up the porch steps, walked past her, Mrs. Parker not moving but blocking with her elbows, just enough to let me know that she'd get me later if she could. The man told Mrs. Parker to stay where she was when I went in the house and climbed up the stairs to my room. I wondered if I should take the radio or not, or if I should take the quilt. I wanted to take something because it was something I wanted to do. I took a picture from the wall, a picture of Mr. and Mrs. Parker with Homer when he was a baby. I put my clothes in a box, and my schoolbooks.

The poor people, the man and the woman, said all they wanted was to give children a chance. "What have they got," they said, "if they don't have anybody?" They said I could be their senior, that they'd never had a senior in high school before, that I could live with them and be spoiled the way they'd spoil children if they'd had any of their own. The poor man looked as if he could shove a horse off a mountain. I remember the man's hands, bigger than my father's. I don't remember the man's name. His wife's name, too, I don't remember. I went into the kitchen, to scrub dishes that were in the sink, but the woman said, "Here now. Don't do that. You go study the way our senior child would do. Go with Miss Doyle. She'll show you to your room. You'll share. She'll share her food, she'll share her room. She said she'd share her bed."

Miss Doyle had a sewn-up harelip and hair straight black with no pretty curl, but she didn't care. She thought she was beautiful. She said she was born that way. She said her mother went to her grave that way. You could see the harelip, the scar going crooked, but you forgot about it right away also. She said, "Don't worry about French, I'll pass you anyway."

The poor people had a baby, too. They liked to get babies from the state. "We like babies best of all. And high school seniors, too," they said. They said, "We'll find you a graduation dress, just don't you worry."

They had a picnic at the church for graduates and Mrs. Parker was in charge, she ran it, showing off her red feather hat, and she had a speech to do, all the important ladies did speeches which graduates had to listen to and pretend to like, which I didn't because I walked out when she started. I got up from my seat and walked toward the door which was in front, to the left of Mrs. Parker, and I felt the people behind me, their eyes, but my heart said, "Go ahead, do it. It's important. Go ahead and do it."

So I walked to the door. I felt Mrs.. Parker's eyes follow, her voice turned when her body did, but she kept on talking as if nothing had happened, as if her eyes were both straight, and I walked out of the church and I was humming. That's when I knew I was pretty and no one could stop me except God.

On graduation night I felt fine. I felt like a million, one in a million, and my face was like Joan Crawford's with high cheekbones and the sucked-in part underneath. I saw my father there, in the gymnasium with folding chairs set up in rows, but I didn't talk to him so he left before it was over. He left as if he had never come. Mrs. Parker wasn't there but Ruth and Homer were, so I pretended they were family, celebrating. We were celebrating. I called the people I lived with 'mother and father' like a graduate would do, and thanked them for the place to live, and I gave Miss Doyle my graduation picture where I looked like Joan Crawford, where I'd used rag strips to make my hair look fancy and Miss Doyle helped me take the rag strips out.

So after graduation, I rode a bus out of town and never went back there and when I was on a sidewalk in another town one afternoon where I was walking with my new friends, a drunk called my name and said, "Can I have a word with you?" When my friends said, "How does he know your name?" I said, "I don't know. He must have seen me when I was coming on the bus from Hollywood."

I said, "I don't know where in the world he would have got my name." I said, "I never met him before."

#35-1460!

Tyrone Symington was the first one who nearly got me to do it. He was a lieutenant in the army and was going overseas, Germany maybe, and everybody at the YW was doing it with guys in uniform. One girl did it, and she never charged. Nobody ever charged. It was kind of patriotic and sad and nobody knew who would get killed or wounded or whether anybody was ever coming back.

You didn't even have to go to a hotel because the Y had little cubbyhole visiting rooms with curtains over the door and if you remembered to bring safety pins, it would take awhile for the desk lady to work her way through the curtains. She never did if you left the light on. Also, she was a stutterer so you could hear her rat-a-tat-tatting through her teeth before she left her stool. Those of us who lived there had to laugh because our families thought purity was guaranteed behind those walls.

I was working in Groom's Stationery Store in an old office building in the center of Boston almost, a couple blocks from South Station Railroad, where servicemen who had an hour to kill came in Groom's and bought I MISS YOU cards with red satin hearts in the middle. Most times they'd be drunk, sailors especially, but nobody minded. They were lonely drunks, not mean.

Mrs. Hamm, my boss, was a fat dumpy woman with a smile as wide as a crossing. She had the funniest kind of humor I ever saw. She could mimic the man calling for Philip Morris or Ishkabibble or anybody, customers even, until it was like when they first walked in. Some days she'd bet me a nickel she could get rid of ten greeting cards that weren't moving. She'd do it, too, sidling up to a customer and saying, "This one is lovely, don't you think?" Or she'd yell out, "Order up Hallmark #35-1460!" Then she'd hand the card to the customer as if, being the last one, they'd surely like to buy it.

Mrs. Hamm understood about my going to South Station for lunch every day. She went with me once, but it made her cry to see all those young boys away from home so I was glad she didn't come after that. She didn't realize about the glamour of being in uniform, traveling all over. South Station had a USO where I'd play Ping-Pong or dance if someone wanted.

South Station was like the mother of the whole world, putting her arms around everyone. It was dark in there, dirty usually, but everybody seemed wired and ready to explode. All that activity made it brighter, like a party; all that hurrying and noise. Important things were going on. If the whole world exploded and if everything ended up dying, I'd have felt right in the middle of it.

At Groom's, Mrs. Hamm ordered greeting cards and I had to do whatever she told me to do—sometimes filling racks, other times climbing up a ladder to get office forms, legal papers, ledger books.

Tyrone came in while I was selling an Esterbrook pen. He said he'd take five if I'd go out to dinner. I said, "Sure." So that's how it started. He had a limp but I didn't mind. He told me he had a plantar wart on the bottom of his foot.

When he left, Dickie Cubble—I called him 'Dickie' because he flirted with everybody—complained to Mrs. Hamm that I pushed Esterbrooks when the mark-up was better on Parkers. He considered himself Groom's expert on fountain pens. He could sell the whole set even though most people just wanted the pen, not the pencil. Mrs. Hamm told me I should call Richard when it looked like there might be a pen sale, so I said, "Sure. I'll be glad to." But I knew I could do great on Esterbrooks. What a name,

Esterbrook. It sounded like a woodsy place, cozy and warm, with pine needles and a hidden pond all silvery and smooth.

That summer and fall Tyrone and I went to dinner, shows, museums. We went dancing once but he got too excited so we didn't do it anymore. I was pushing up close, nuzzling, when he pushed me away. I could tell what was happening. When he shoved me back, I stepped on his sore foot so we talked about that instead. We didn't go swimming for the same reason. His sister, Mary, was seventeen, same as I was, and he said if any guy messed with her before marriage, he'd kill him. When I knew for sure he meant it, I teased him to get him all hot and bothered.

He was boring in an older sort of way, but I liked being seen with him because he looked beautiful in his uniform, the silver bar on his shoulder, the officer's cap. The plantar wart gave him an injured look. People notice things like that. Even though he didn't wear any ribbons to say where he'd been, I knew they figured he'd been wounded overseas. He didn't mind them thinking that, either. I could tell because whenever people stopped to shake his hand or grab his arm and said, "Good show, soldier," he always smiled and said, "Thank you, Sir," or "Thank you, Ma'am," if it happened to be a woman.

I knew I could trust him. I liked kissing him good-night even though he didn't open his mouth. And he didn't want me to, either. A couple of times I kind of groaned and let my mouth fall open as if I didn't realize, but he pushed on my jaw until it closed.

He hated me going to South Station on my lunch hour and was always trying to get me to promise I wouldn't. He said it made me look like a pick-up. I promised I wouldn't but I went anyway.

Ten days before Christmas, Mr. Groom gave a party for his employees and I invited Tyrone. We danced half of the first dance and drank Champagne and at the end of the party, Mr. Groom gave everyone a turkey. Mr. Widensee was the store manager so he got the biggest. We sang, "Thank you, thank you, Mr. Groom," until we sounded like Handel's *Messiah* with seven Hallelujahs.

I gave Tyrone the turkey for his mother since he was going home anyway. Also, he put his hand on my breasts. Not bare, but over my sweater. It surprised him, I could tell, but we pretended it hadn't happened. He gave me a $50 savings bond for Christmas, which I cashed in for $37.50.

The last week of December we were working late on inventory in Groom's store, counting pens, pencils, taking tallies, when Mr. Widensee called me into the basement. He was an old man like my father, not mean or anything but scrawny looking. I never paid him much attention because Mrs. Hamm did the bossing as far as I was concerned.

Mr. Widensee was like a king. He always got the biggest turkeys and he was the one who signed the checks. He never asked me to dance at the Christmas party, but I didn't feel bad because he didn't ask Mrs. Hamm, either. He had a wife with bony elbows, and her shoes squeaked when she walked. She was the kind you stay away from before she starts yelling.

When I got down in the basement, I could hear Mr. Widensee calling but I couldn't see him. "Back here," he said, so I went farther into the stacks of papers, forms, greeting card boxes, and there he was. He grabbed my breasts and started to squeeze them. It hurt but it made me mad so I bit his hand. He tried to pull me closer, to push his body next to mine.

"I'll tell," I said. "I'll tell Mrs. Hamm and Dickie Cubble." His eyes faded back into his head. His face was twisted and turned almost purple like he might be having a heart attack.

"They'll call the police," I said.

"If I let you go, will you promise not to tell?" He pushed away a little bit.

"I promise."

So he let me go and I went upstairs and told Mrs. Hamm and Dickie Cubble and they agreed I should go on home. Dickie told Mrs. Hamm I shouldn't come back because I was always causing trouble and Mrs. Hamm said, "Well, we'll see."

When I got back to the Y, there was a message to call Tyrone, which I did. I told him about Mr. Widensee and he said, "That's what you get for going to South Station. Everybody thinks you're a pick-up." I started to cry so he said, "Never mind. We'll talk about it New Year's Eve." That made me cry even harder. The only thing that made me feel better was that I was really crying. Just like the people at South Station.

New Year's Eve it was snowing so hard cars were stopped in the streets. Everyone was celebrating. It was as if we'd already won the war. Tyrone and I ran all the way to Mechanic's Street Station, even though he kept slowing down because of his sore foot, and we ran back, right down the middle of the street. We were throwing snowballs when someone in the North Tower rang the bells. When I hit Tyrone in the eye with a snowball, he rubbed my face in a snowbank but suddenly he was kissing me instead.

We went inside the Y to a cubbyhole room where he said he loved me. He said it was our last date, that he was confined to the base until further orders.

"Oh no!" I said. "If you leave, I'll have no one!" I started to cry again and I could tell he liked that. Suddenly, I really didn't want him to go. His hands were on my sweater, then under, and then he was crying, too. He would have gone all the way, I know, but he couldn't because of what he'd said about his sister. I would have done it anyway, but the lady from the desk was by the curtains saying, "You f-f-forgot the safety p-p-pins."

So he left. He promised he'd write; that if I was still a virgin when he got back, he'd marry me. When I went up to my room, I prayed, but praying wasn't the same thing as loving. It was as if I were praying for the soldiers I played Ping-Pong with and the sailors I sold cards to. It was as if I were standing in South Station and the trains weren't running anymore.

Tyrone never wrote while he was overseas. Finally, his sister, Mary, called to say he lost his leg and was being sent back to the States. She said I could see him at Battle Creek if I wanted. After she hung up, I thought about visiting him but decided not to. I had lost my job at Groom's, partly because of Dickie Cubble when I sold all the Parker Pen sets in one day and partly because of Mr. Widensee, who couldn't stand the sight of me. Also, I had to go to college so I could start a new life. They said I could work my way through.

I kept thinking about Tyrone's leg and wondering if it was the one with the wart. When Tyrone finally called, he sounded like an old man. I knew he was going to ask me to marry him so I told him I wasn't a virgin; that I had to go to college right away. He said he didn't care. Maybe it was for the best, he said, and wished me luck. I wanted to tell him I loved him but if I did, it would be for keeps and I couldn't do that.

Then he said, "Hey, kid, you still there?" He said, "My plantar wart is gone," and I told him I thought so. He promised to write because he had five Esterbrooks to use up but said I didn't have to answer unless I wanted. I told him I would, that we could still be friends. He wrote once after that and I wrote back but then I never heard from him again.

Do It

I think, do it do it do it.

He limps and falls into the drapes.

I dress in the dark—my black dress, imitation pearls. I put a flashlight in my pocket.

I cross the gutter on the way to my friends' place and I feel my nipples pucker. I hop over the gutter.

I run into the lighted place with its drapes drawn against the world. It is good to be with friends. We dance. We sing. We drink Champagne. We are in the center of everything important. My boyfriend tweaks my nipples and pinches my behind. Sailors come and go in this town. Their ships leave after dark for places far away.

"Listen, do you want to see a suicide?" I don't know why I say that. I just say it, is all.

"Let's go see!" my boyfriend yells, and suddenly the lighted place is empty and we are all running down the street. It is very dark but I lead the way. I have my flashlight. I say, "This way, this way," as if I am an usher in an all-night movie.

We enter through golden drapes. My father is on the floor. His false teeth are in a pool of vomit, spread as if making fun. A rope is coiled with one loop over the door knob, a chair tipped on its back. Something went wrong, or right; who knows for sure?

My friends know for sure. They say, "He's not dead, you whore."

The Point

While the dishes drain, you lick a finger and wipe spit on each dish. It's possible you have a terrible disease and everyone will die, then God will really be sorry.

You wake in the morning with plaster weighing you down. The ceiling is falling. As you roll off your pallet, four yelling children burst into the room, except for the littlest boy who can't yell because he has a thumb in his mouth, two fingers of the same hand stuck up his nose and the other hand busy with his dingle.

You say, "What's happening?" The children surge forward as if you're an animal escaped from a circus and you can maybe do tricks. When they jump on the pallet, dust from the plaster flies in the air. You leave the room, coughing and choking. The Missus (you don't know her name) is in the kitchen banging pans. No food on the table, Uncle Harry and your father sit stiff as dummies, their eyes bugging out like eyes on a frog. They mumble instead of talk, as if they've forgotten the language. The house sighs.

"What's that?" you ask, thinking God listened after all and is into something special, shaking up the world. What He had in mind could be better than what you thought and you start to thank Him, thinking your life is beginning right this minute. You run to the door in case He's outside waiting and you see what you didn't notice in the night. You'd climbed a ladder to get in the house but you were too tired to think about strangeness. In the daytime you see that the house is on stilts. Outside, it is raining. The children move on to the living room and begin jumping to see if the house will tip over. You jump, too, until The Missus appears switching a flyswatter. "Damn kids," she says. "Damn kids." The flyswatter makes red marks on their bare legs. "Get out in the kitchen and help," she says. "Get the kids dressed for school and don't flush the toilet."

You wonder if you're going to school, too, but don't say anything because you'd rather stay at home and watch the house move. Uncle Harry says, "dead horse," and your father laughs a wheezing laugh that ends up in a cough. Plaster dust drifts into the kitchen, making the room seem like it's in a fog. Your father says, "Had to cut their legs off, eh?" and continues laughing. Outside, the movers are cranking up the house. The children run back to the living room to jump some more. The Missus says, "Get the kids out, Harry," then goes into her bedroom and slams the door. Uncle Harry follows the children outside as if he's on a leash. Your father is on the floor. He's wet himself and his urine looks to you cold.

You watch from the point where the ladder was and you see men on machines. The men wear yellow slickers and heavy boots with cleats. You know they think everybody is outside, that the house is empty. You wish your father worked with them so you'd get to wear his slicker when he got home.

The men start to yell and the house goes on forward.

Let. Me. Hide. Myself. In. Theeeee.

Megan said she'd drive me up there in her Rolls, the '67 Silver Ghost, with mahogany and leather everything inside (she was into style that year), to start me off right in the big five-oh year, the first part of the second half of the century of my life.

We were going to stay at Ellen's even though Ellen wasn't there, nor were her kids, but Esther, the maid from Colombia who came into the country on a Billy Graham crusade, was. She'd paid a thousand dollars to marry an American and she'd gone to Canada (she said) on a honeymoon with twenty other Colombian women who'd married the same man. Esther said her marriage was consummated, but when she said it, it sounded to me as if she didn't know what she was talking about.

Megan picked me up in the Rolls, her hair piled high, Big Hair kids called it, three wigs to make her look taller, which she already was. Megan was a former Playboy Bunny. She had an exquisite face with alabaster complexion, wide violet eyes, extra long false eyelashes with penciled-in markings to 'make them stand out,' she said. She drew lashes on her eyelids, too, which made her look as if she blinked twice every time.

She had her own way of doing things, and so did I. We were best friends although how that came about is another story. It had to do with pigeon shit on my car and a crazed German Shepherd at a gas station in Indiana.

I'm older than Megan by fifteen years but she promised she could make me over into a knockout to start me off right on the first day of the rest of my life.

Megan's not the greatest driver in the world. She tends to waver from one side of the road to the other. Drivers give her a wide berth, letting her have the whole middle lane because of the Rolls.

At the Oasis she told the young boy who waited on us to give her five. The kid spent ten minutes cleaning the windshield and twenty minutes polishing the headlights with Megan in the driver's seat saying, "I love it. I love it."

The kid forgot to collect until I reminded him, and then he was at the driver's window, saying, "Jesus, Lady, you sure are lucky with a beaut like this. Do you mind if I ask how much it cost?" He looked as if he'd crawl into her lap if she asked him to. Megan laughed and said, "Oh you darling boy."

When we got to Ellen's, Esther let us in but didn't look too happy about having us there while Ellen was out of town. She showed us where we could sleep and then went back to her piano playing on the third floor where the piano had been pulleyed up through a window, ruining the siding, which had had to be replaced. She was practicing church songs, making the pauses so long while she hunted down the keys that it took her thirty minutes to get through the first line. Rock. Of. Ages. Cleft. For. Me. Let. Me. Hide. Myself. In. Theeeee.

You could hear the note-pause-pause-note, sour as a crate of grapefruit, drift down from the third floor, down the sidewalk. We could tell she was annoyed before she opened the door because of all the keys she'd banged on. For a decent upright Billy Graham Christian convert, she wasn't all that nice.

When we got inside the house, Megan and I had to make our own drinks, find our own ice cubes. Esther was in one of her *no speaka An-glai-sa* moods so we had to make do with cheese and crackers, although Megan did find some Beluga caviar way back on a shelf. Megan got out her carpetbag and did my face, including etched lashes on my eyelids and painted-on lipstick with a cupid's bow, like the ad for MAGICKISS. She said I looked gorgeous. I decided to not look in the mirror but to trust to fate about this first day of the rest of my life.

"So," Megan said. "Now what?" Even though we were a lot different, we were really close friends.

Esther's piano playing was beginning to bother us, she was banging on the keys harder, as if to make up for the pauses. Also, Ellen's liquor cabinet was practically bare, so we decided to check out the town before we came on back to Ellen's house to sleep.

We went to Mushroom's first, a place that's closed now, but used to have great Cape Cod potato chips. We had a couple of drinks there, then realized we'd better get something to eat, so we paid the bill and headed for Fiona's house. She was always home and she liked us.

Megan backed up on the curb when she pulled out of the parking place, left a skid mark on the sidewalk.

Fiona had a house set back in the woods. The thing I liked best was her potato whip that hung in the entry between her living room and her dining room. That whip was five feet long and swung back and forth if you bumped it. Fiona wasn't expecting us, but she invited us into her bar room and mixed us drinks. She gave me a Kleenex to wipe off a beauty mark Megan had pasted on my right cheek, a little round dot. She said she and her husband had plans for dinner and would be leaving as soon as he came home. Which turned out to be a lie because when he came home, he hugged Megan like he never wanted to let her go, and asked us to stay for dinner. But Megan and I got Fiona's point and left shortly after that. Megan backed into a rosebush on the way out.

So there we were. No place to go and we knew we couldn't go back on the expressway with all we'd had to drink and it was too early, we thought, to go back to Ellen's with Esther playing the piano. The Little Brown Church pause pause pause didn't sound like having a very good time.

By this time, Megan and I were on a tear and restless about what to do next. As Megan drove, I noticed how cars slowed down when they came toward us. They didn't pass us from behind, either, no matter how slow we were going. Somewhere in there, I noticed how dark it was getting and that's when Megan realized she was driving with no lights on. I can imagine what people thought when they saw this gray ghost coming at them. At the time, to tell you the truth, neither of us gave a damn. It was like, here we were, grown-ups, married and mothers, still having fun.

Megan was crossing over the yellow line down the middle of the road a lot, so I was glad when we saw a place, STOP AND SOCK, and saw that it was open, which most places weren't this time of night. It looked like a country club, a golf place because of its name, so Megan parked in the parking lot and we went inside.

The men seemed friendly enough. I think I bought a fishing pole from one of them, although I don't have it around to prove it. I remember bragging about a fish I caught, a northern pike, and I remember showing the men at the bar how I put my fingers in its eyes to blind it so I could take the hook out. But things are vague about what happened there. I remember playing the slot machines, and I remember falling against a machine next to mine and making the machine tilt, which made the man playing it very angry. And I remember falling down and someone picking me up.

All of a sudden Megan turned mean. You know she had a terrible childhood. I think her childhood was worse than mine because her parents put her in jail when she was only fourteen when she didn't behave the way they thought a good Catholic girl should. They put her in a women's detention ward with tough street babes who ran their hands over her face and squeezed her breasts. That was before she became a Bunny and learned how to handle hands that were put where you didn't want them put. My childhood was moving to different cities all the time, and looking in bars for my father. And waiting there until he finished whatever he was doing before walking him home. That was my job as a kid: walking my father home.

Megan threatened to call her uncle when they cut off her drinks at the bar. The name she gave her uncle made the men freeze because he was a famous hit man. Still, they refused to give her any more drinks and the first thing I knew, Megan was gone, and they were turning off the lights, and when I went out to the parking lot, there was no one there, no one and no cars, except this old car and a man standing next to me who kept picking me up when I fell, and telling me that I was too nice a lady to be falling down all the time, and what were all those marks on my eyelids and where did I live? He said he'd take me home because, obviously, my friend had left and I had to get out of there, because I shouldn't have been there in the first place. He was short and held his hands up to his mouth, which made him seem shy and vulnerable. And kind. I liked that he seemed kind.

It was the first time in my life I really felt old. I felt that my bones were breaking, and my heart. I remember going to this place and falling down in a parking lot, and him picking me up a few times, and then we were going to the front steps of this place, with large oak doors all carved and decorated with women lolling about with their arms up over their heads, and lying down, and there were lions and there were gargoyles, and a woman opened the door about six inches, there was a bolt on the door, and she said, "Yes, Sir. We are open."

Duck Blind

The camp was asleep and night came alive, dark folded round her, keeping her company. Her name was Mary Rhinegold and her back ached, her feet hurt. She was incontinent. "You are incontinent," her doctor had said, putting a name to it. She thought he'd said she was to go to the continent and imagined Italy, maybe Paris, one of those places. "Surely you're joking, doctor," she'd said.

"I think not," he'd said. "Get the old-fashioned cloth ones. They'll hold up nicely."

She chose Birch Point Camp, the place where they'd taken the children for years. She arrived late afternoon, and now, early morning, she decided that after this trip, a mission, she wanted only city lights, gay nights, and low throaty jazz, glasses and glasses of wine. Outside, the loons, those crazy loons, had at it with their loony cries, *ha-oo-oo* and falsetto wails, the barking in flight.

She bent down, turned on a valve, let the gas heater suck air, then scratched a wooden match against a square of sandpaper which had been nailed to a wooden post. She lit the heater and the stove, then put on a kettle of water. The coffee looked black and strong. Later, in the duck blind, she would make more coffee, mix in a raw egg, the way, her son once said, Marines made coffee in Vietnam.

She pulled on two pair of pants, one pair of wool socks, hiking boots. "Work from the bottom up," her husband had always said. He'd taught her to fish though, not hunt. She'd never hunted in her life. Darly would be amazed, she thought, missing him, wondering why she'd lasted so long and he hadn't.

She continued: three sweatshirts, mackintosh jacket of black and red-checked wool, matching hat with visor and ear flaps. Everyone in the family had worn the jacket: sons, daughter, husband. Once the mack had saved Darly's sanity, the time they were stranded by ten-foot waves and couldn't cross the channel in Rainey Lake. God, how long ago? Ten years? Fifteen? Darly had had a tic douloureux attack and the mack kept his face protected from the sharp Canadian wind. They'd hunkered down on an island, waiting all night for the winds to calm.

Well, they used to be here and now they're not, Mary thought. And that's that. She tucked her thin white hair under a scarf, pulled on the mack hat, gloves, then headed out of her cabin.

Forgot to drink the coffee. Lordy. Lordy. She returned to the cabin, slammed the door. Drank the coffee and listened as waves slapped the shore, heard stones move underneath the lake, heard the reedy notes of a bobolink. "Who says I'm deaf?" she said. She studied the slate blue sky, thunder clouds rolling in. The duck blind will be cold. No matter. Nothing matters anymore. "Sorry, God," she said, "I didn't mean that." She wanted to tell Him more, tried to remember what it was. Had to do with her children, how she'd loved them. "Oh well," she said. "Whatever."

There's that damn song again, *Sweet Hour of Prayer*, trilling.

She turned off the gas heater, shut off the burner. Remembers: Don't slam the door, don't wake the campers next cabin over. Thought: Damn fools. Poker all night. Would've ruined everything if they'd seen me leave. No one goes fishing alone.

They'd been to Birch Point many times. First family there in fact: man, wife, and children at an all-male camp. The men had resented it, their being there, but Darly didn't mind. That first year, the guide had thought it funny, his mixed party with a woman and little kids bringing in the biggest catch. Over the years, going back to Birch Point, the guide taught the boys how to fillet, herself and her daughter how to handle a motor.

The children were in their thirties and forties now, all grown.

114

Last year the children had told her she mustn't think of going to Birch Point in her condition.

She'd called last October for May reservations. "Four adults," she'd said. "Two children." But no one knew, not even the grand-children.

When she'd arrived at Birch Point, they'd expected six in the party for cabin eight.

"Family's coming later today," she'd announced at the lodge. The guide's son ran the camp now. His kids called her Mamaw.

"Wanted to take my time traveling so I came along early," she'd said. She'd registered for the duck blind at Footprint Lake, reserved a boat, motor, full tank of gas. So early in the season, scarcely anyone would be on the lake to notice she was alone.

Fishing rods and reels, bait, tackle box, Remington, all in the trunk of her car. She'd already planned how to unload the trunk. Packed loose were: bucket to sit on, skillet, coffee pot, fishing gear, waders, the Remington. She must remember to not wade deep. Darly had done that while portaging once. His waders had filled, anchoring him to the lake bottom. Their sons had pulled him out but it wasn't easy, and they'd had to slice the waders with fillet knives.

She divided into two duffel bags enough supplies to last a life-time. Number one bag contained peanut oil, flour and cornmeal mix, salt and pepper, spatula, coffee, a sharp knife. She slipped a raw egg sealed in a Ziploc baggie into the mack pocket. Number two duffel held wool socks, tennis shoes, more diapers, soap, a thermal blanket. Extra shells for the Remington were in her tackle box, along with Bufferin just in case. Never know what might happen. Darly had taught her that.

The drive to Footprint was slow because Mary wanted to remember everything: those tall pines with hundreds of years of brown needles on the floor of the forest, white birch with its bark the white of an egg, the boulder in the road you watched for. She shifted into low gear to climb the hill. A view of Footprint Lake spilled out at the top of the hill like a giant moccasin. Indians from the Cree tribe had named the lake; Footprint, the perfect name. She'd fished in all the coves, found secret walleye holes, caught a seven-pounder but lost it when her daughter dropped the net.

Waves slapped the dock in quiet splashes. Her boat was ready in the water. The motor was in place, tipped forward to protect its blades. She knew she'd have to row out to the end of the pier before she could start the motor. "Can do," she said. She headed the car into a parking space along the beach then backed up close to the shoreline to unload. Good. The sand was firm; she won't get stuck. She moved her gear to the boat, struggling with the two duffel bags which would balance the load. She'd taken two Bufferin. If she's lucky, her back will hold.

She wore two diapers, already damp. No matter. Later she'll build a fire. No time now to change. She must settle in the blind before morning light comes. She must blend in with the bulrushes, the marsh grass. The colors of the mack might alert the birds, but she had no choice because she needed the warmth. When she gets chilled, she piddles more. She's learned to stay warm, reasonably dry. She'd not counted on incontinence. "Bastard," she said, blaming the doctor. But in a practical way, clean and dry, diapers doubled as tourniquets, wiping cloths, handkerchiefs. Or, knotted and wet, protected her head from the sun.

She loaded the boat, pulled the car back into the parking slot, slid the key under the front floor mat. A squirrel chattered on the rim of a trash can. The wind had died down. A gray morning, four o'clock.

She twisted her bad ankle getting into the boat, forgetting that aluminum is slippery. She rowed to the end of the pier, dipping oars in gentle circular motions. She was pleased with how easily the boat slid through the water. The lake so clear that when she looked down, she could see the bottom. Pebbles and rocks looked like washed bones. At the end of the pier, she drew in the oars and placed them in their locks. She pulled on the choke, squeezed the feedline to the gasoline and hoped she didn't have to suck the tube to prime it.

She pulled the starter rope once and the motor purred. "Sweet hour," she said. "Of prayer." She waved to a lone man fishing off the pier, then pointed her boat out toward the main body of the lake.

She took the lake at full speed, although 25 horsepower wasn't much. Cabins along the shore were empty, too early in the season for campers. She slowed down when she rounded a bend, remembering the raggedy-edged boulders just below the surface in the narrow pass.

The boat drifted over the boulders while she guided with oars. The lake was deep enough this year; a blessing. A deer was feeding offshore. A heron stood on one leg. She smiled, pleased. She rubbed her ankle, which had begun to swell.

The rapids were a piece of cake. She'd watched her boys and Darly pass through them, going uphill to the next lake, speeding down coming back, a narrow pass with high black boulders on either side. She'd always thought they'd pulled off magic, shooting the rapids, but now found it was all a matter of guiding the boat through the narrow pass. She wasn't as strong as she used to be but no matter. Determination was what counted. She gunned the motor and shot up into the next lake, Lake Despair. She'd wondered often about that name. How did the Cree know that word? Had they tried to cross the lake and a wind came up? Lake Hope, she called it now.

The duck blind was across from Teepee Point. She'd seen the blind many times. Two by fours and planks of wood covered with tree limbs, bulrushes. Someone had placed an imitation mallard near the opening of the blind, a marker. The wooden duck was tied with fish line and floated in the water, bobbing on waves.

She cut the motor then drifted toward the blind. A wind came up and she had a little trouble guiding the boat onto shore. Weeds and water lily vines strangled the motor blades. She pulled the motor up out of the water then stood in the boat to guide it with an oar. She could put only a little weight on her sprained ankle. Easy does it. She thought of the heron.

A platform the width of the blind rose out of the water. She decided to leave the duffels in the boat, took the rods, tackle, tackle box, and the Remington. She'd been told the Remington must stay dry; that it had a kick to it when fired. She knew she'd deal with the kick when the time came.

It took longer than she expected—moving gear with a swollen ankle. She swallowed two more Bufferin, using the clear lake water to wash them down. She knew she was running late. She shoved aside branches on a log inside the blind then sat on an upended bucket. She baited her line with a Red Devil, which she'd repainted with bright red fingernail polish. She loaded the Remington, placed it across her lap, then dropped bait in the water. She hadn't figured out what she'd do if she had a bite. She hoped the fish would wait because she wanted to think about how she'd handle both the gun and the line. She wished she'd brought a thermos. Oh well.

She waited. Outside the blind, the wooden duck bobbled in the water, up and down and up and down. It could use another coat of paint. She checked her bait then changed to a jig, going for walleye. Walleye were gentler to handle because they nibbled rather than grabbed. Northerns grab and can take your arm off. Northerns were called snakes, but still, their fillets were flaky and fresh. They used to eat them for shore lunch, picking out bones with their fingers. Didn't use forks, just hands and fingers.

She waited. The sun came up quickly, a burst of fire. The lake was azure blue, white caps in the distance. A single gull circled the blind, a scout, the lead gull that checked out food for the gang.

She waited. She was warmer, her ankle a dull ache. She knew that death was a buzzard with large flapping wings, a full yellow beak, legs outstretched beneath his body, claws extended to grab its prey. In dreams, which she read as warnings, she'd seen the buzzard every night since last October.

The gun was cocked and ready. She'd take aim and shoot that buzzard with all the might that was in her. She wanted to see Paris again, listen to jazz, drink more wine.

She sighted down the Remington for practice. A seagull's belly fit in the squared-off patch along the barrel. She'd never shoot the gull because gulls take care of their own. She was waiting for the buzzard and would kill it with a perfect shot. She was as ready as she'd ever be.

It became warmer with the sun shining, so she took off the mackintosh hat and jacket and placed them on the platform. She knotted a diaper and draped it over her head to protect her bald spots. Her hair had always been thin. She parted the flap on the blind so she could have a wider view of the sky. Buzzards were easy prey. You aimed straight and fired then fired again if you had to.

She sat on the bucket, her diapers soaked. She raised up her leg with the swollen ankle so that it rested on a forked branch.

Incontinent, indeed. She was just getting started. Life was just beginning. Paris was just around the corner and nothing could stop her now.

Sweet hour, she thought. And waited.

Pumpkins

"What have you been doing?" she asked. We were talking on the phone, so I read to her the poem I'd been working on, making my voice slide over the rough spots I'd not worked out yet, smoothing them over, secretly proud of the 'full moon casting shadows/ on cornfields/ the windmill off in the distance/ lumber piles/ in a meadow.'

She said, "Look, you're painting a pretty picture, you're setting up an easel and doing water colors of a nice little sunset …"

"Full moon," I said. I hadn't even got to the windburned leaves on transplanted saplings yet, the ones we bought off the motorcycle gang that drove up from southern Illinois where they'd probably ripped the trees off a subdivision down there, the same way people rip off evergreens out here in Homer Township. Half those saplings are dead now, and I'd sure like to zap those guys with their black tee shirts and broken-down cowboy boots and their red hot mama with a silver bow in her hair. Their cycles were in the back of the semi they drove up in and the mama was sleeping in the cab. My husband Ollie said they gave him a deal he couldn't refuse.

"So full moon," she said. "I know you'll EVENTUALLY tell me something new and funny and mysterious …"

"It gets worse," I promised. "I tell about wanting to call this place Honky Haven." But we ended up naming it Windmill Acres because the building and the subdividing was a family affair and my kids don't much like my smart mouth.

"So how worse?" she asked.

"I was going to tell about Ollie going fishing with that Winston Salem guy and his son. You remember, that sharp-looking guy who nearly did an ad on a horse for that cigarette company? I was going to make it a villanelle."

Silence.

"Well, Ollie went to Canada with Winston Salem and his son, name of Tarr, ugly as Winston Salem is good-looking, and Tarr's still a badmouth skinny little kid to me, even though he's six foot now, and has pockmarks all over his face like he was hit with gravel from one of those trucks that go flying by."

"Flying by?" she said.

I waited."He badmouths his sister, Ollie said. He said that Tarr says every woman has nookie he'd like to ram, even the Indian ones at Indian Village, the place along the shore up in Canada where Ollie and Tarr and Winston Salem caught nothing but snags."

"Did he?"

"Did who?"

"That Tarr person. Ram the Indians."

"Ollie didn't say."

Dead silence on the phone.

"So think about that town you moved back to, Lock Port," she said. "Think about the lock and the port and how the town is dead but there are all those subdivisions going up. And tell about that front lawn with the plastic Mother Goose with the ducklings and how they wore yellow slickers when it rained because the owner thought he was a weatherman. Tell about that," she said.

Who cares about ducks wearing yellow slickers? I'm looking for a poem here. Maybe a story if I get lucky.

"Well," I said, "the Texaco plant doesn't smell as bad as it did when it was operating, spewing out sewer gas or something. But no one wanted to talk about the smell, and when I mentioned it once, the smell, when I lived here before and was on a bowling team, they almost balled me up and rolled me down the alley because that was what kept the town alive, they said. That smell keeps us going; what are you, some kind of snob? they said. It's closed down now, the Texaco, and half the townfolk are out of work. But they still string up the Christmas lights along those empty oil drums, along those dead power lines."

"That's pretty good," she said. "The part about Christmas lights meaning life and the power lines symbolizing death. Terrific."

"Well. Yeah." But I didn't want her to hang up, so I said, "Tarr is mean, Ollie said, and works for the Phengston brothers on a farm where they grow pumpkins. And what Tarr does is he builds the spook houses and the squash house and a couple more scary houses, and it takes four months to get it all set up, getting ready for the whole month of October when they make ten thousand dollars selling popcorn and pumpkins to kids bussed in from the city, and people bussed from nursing homes, and more bussed in from Manteno if they can get a driver who isn't crazy, in yellow busses. And Tarr does the sound effects with hard rock hooked up to his stereo, and the farmers hate it because of the traffic jams but they love it, too, because Phengston's pumpkins made them famous, they've put Lock Port on the map and now the farmers who aren't subdividing are growing pumpkins."

"Do that one," she said, "about the pumpkins."

When she hung up, I thought about ending up in a nuthouse with Tarr's hard rock blaring, the kind of music that goes right to your center until you feel locked up with no air to breathe, you're trapped inside, and even if you could get out you'd never be able to leave town because of the traffic, the people looking for a piece of Americana to take home and put in their windows, a pumpkin with a face cut in it and a candle stuck in the middle.

Last night the full moon
made shadows in the
cornfields.

Up close, I saw
a windmill.

I saw lumber piled high.

I saw saplings bend
and I heard windburned
leaves;

and, from the deck
of the new house
where I live,

I heard semitrucks.
I heard the drivers shift
gears, cursing the

back roads, too narrow
to pass a farmer's
truck

loaded with a buzz saw
for cutting down
trees,

a wheelbarrow for
carrying pumpkins
off the fields.

I drove by the Phengstons' pumpkin fields, slowing down to
see what they looked like, imagining perfect little pumpkins the
size of those Hallowe'en orange candies, soft, with bright green
leaves. But all I saw were what looked like empty fields a farmer
had let go fallow. We'd had no rain all spring and now the fields
were nothing but dry dirt with layers of dust.

I pulled the car off the road, walked into the weeds, and
shaded my eyes. There was a truck out there and a trailer, but the
fields looked dead and there weren't any pumpkins. The fields

were dead, the town was dead, and I was sorry I hadn't gone rappelling with my husband, or called a friend, or done something to get me out of the rut I was in. Nothing was alive in me and I felt the kind of dead a woman feels when her children have grown and moved away and the marriage has lost its spark.

Then I heard the buzzing of a distant motor so I turned round and saw the dust and then, up closer, as it came round the bend, a motorcycle, and closer still, I saw it was Tarr riding without a helmet. He was standing up, practicing a stunt as if he were riding a horse in a circus, or the way kids used to do wheelies in our drive. He came to a stop just as it looked as if he might fly over the top of my car.

At that moment, I thought of Tarr as I had known him when I'd been friends with his mother in the olden days before I'd had the affair I've not told a living soul about, with his father, Winston Salem. I've scarcely admitted the affair to myself let alone dealt with the guilt I've had toward Winston Salem's wife, Tarr's mother, and Ollie, my husband. Tarr had been the bratty little kid his mother brought along to visit, asking could he take a dip in our pool. "Just a little dip," his mother always said. "We won't stay long." But she'd stayed and we'd had a few beers and the beers had tasted cool and good, and finally, when we'd had several, we could take the kids or leave them. We could take them or let them go.

Tarr was a smartass kid, as if he knew everything his father did and everything his mother did, too, and their friends. When he spoke to me back then, Tarr had a look that made me feel as if he knew what his father and I did, and would tell, if I didn't pay attention. He was an ugly kid even then, Tarr was, his eyes never going in the same direction, his arms long and his skinny legs going up and up to his balls which were always half hanging out because of the way he hitched his trunks up after getting out of the pool.

"Wanna screw?" he said now, grinning that knowing ugly grin, his eyeteeth still not yanked out the way they should have been when he was little.

His question made me laugh, knowing him when he was knee-high, and then sleeping with his father and pretending to be his mother's best friend, wondering all those years how much he knew. I couldn't stop laughing, which made him laugh, too, and he climbed off the Harley, kicked out the kickstand, and waded into the weeds next to me, both of us howling idiots now, standing in the weeds, getting bitten by mosquitoes and laughing our fool heads off.

"Well, hell," he said when we finally stopped. "Wanna go for a ride then?"

"Sure," I said and climbed on in back and, hugging him round the waist, gripping hard because I'd never ridden a motorcycle before, wondering what in the world he thought of me, an old woman now by his standards, no longer fooling around, not even with Ollie, except on birthdays and holidays, and only then if we both felt like it and weren't too sleepy.

He crisscrossed the pumpkin fields, the dust kicking up behind us until we were in another world where the dust made me gasp until I could scarcely breathe, and the Harley went airborne sometimes, flying through space. We kicked up field stones and dead old vines, and the sky turned brown with our riding. The truck in the fields, and the trailer flew by, and the back roads. We flew through Lock Port, past the Texaco plant, past the green lawn with Mother Goose in front. Then back to the pumpkin fields again, flying across them, until Tarr pulled up the front wheels, doing wheelies, and I nearly flew off backwards but I didn't, and we came to a dead stop next to the trailer which Tarr had a key for. He lived there, he said, and we rushed inside, me still flying. We ripped off our clothes scarcely thinking of our bodies and plugged into each other and pumped away, like doing wheelies or rappelling against sheer rock, my head lighting up like the Texaco plant at Christmastime, Lock Port and my world coming alive, coming alive again, and it wasn't even my birthday or a holiday, and this kid inside me was better than anything I'd ever known, better than his father, I told him.

"That's what you get for coming back," he said when we finally separated, rolled over, drank a beer, smoked a joint which I'd never done before and had always said 'say no' to my kids about; but here I was, doing it, doing everything I never thought I'd be doing again in this town.

And later, when I got home and Ollie saw me, he said, "Hey, kiddo, is it your birthday or something?"

And I said, "No. It's yours, I think. Let's celebrate."